# Productivity

## The Economy | Key Ideas

These short primers introduce students to the core concepts, theories and models, both new and established, heterodox and mainstream, contested and accepted, used by economists and political economists to understand and explain the workings of the economy.

*Published*

*Behavioural Economics*
Graham Mallard

*Degrowth*
Giorgos Kallis

*The Gig Economy*
Alex De Ruyter and Martyn Brown

*The Informal Economy*
Colin C. Williams

*The Living Wage*
Donald Hirsch and Laura Valadez-Martinez

*Marginalism*
Bert Mosselmans

*Productivity*
Michael Haynes

*The Resource Curse*
S. Mansoob Murshed

# Productivity

Michael Haynes

**agenda**
publishing

First published in 2020 by Agenda Publishing

Agenda Publishing Limited
The Core
Bath Lane
Newcastle Helix
Newcastle upon Tyne
NE4 5TF
www.agendapub.com

ISBN 978-1-78821-146-8 (hardcover)
ISBN 978-1-78821-147-5 (paperback)

**British Library Cataloguing-in-Publication Data**
A catalogue record for this book is available from the British Library

Typeset by JS Typesetting Ltd, Porthcawl, Mid Glamorgan
Printed and bound in the UK by TJ International

# Contents

# Preface

Productivity is one of the most important concepts in economics, but it took a long time to get established. The first use of the word in *The Times* seems to have been in 1858. Nearly seven years later it appeared for a second time in a discussion from the great chemist Liebig. He was asking whether the productivity of the soil could (in addition to using farmyard manure, the ground bone dust of animals and humans, Peruvian guano and new chemicals) be improved by the use of "Metropolitan sewage" (*The Times*, 25 January 1865). The real world of productivity can take us to many such strange places, but these often get elided in the discussions of economists. Since 1945 productivity has become something of an obsession, so much so that when it was suggested that I write a book on productivity my immediate reaction was that a good introduction must already exist. But while books have discussed different aspects of "productivity", there have been few attempts to draw these strands together in a single work focused on productivity and the economy.

What qualifications do I have to try to produce such a synthesis? At first I thought none. Then I realized that in one way or another the question of productivity has been a thread running through much of what I have taught and researched over the years.

One aspect of this has been my interest in the patterns of the global economy, their history and the work of Angus Maddison. I first encountered Maddison as a result of an interest in Russia and Japan, about which he wrote a pioneering comparative study. I followed his work as he began to create a database of global gross domestic product (GDP) pushing the figures back as far as he could. Today, partly in his footsteps, we have a variety of databases that contain a mass of historical and contemporary data that feed into our understanding of productivity. I draw on some of them here and there is a short note on them at the start of the bibliography to guide readers.

Beyond Maddison I have been lucky to be able to teach about and research a wide variety of countries. Sometimes this was by choice, sometimes it was just to survive in the UK's unstable higher education sector. But whether by choice or necessity, I took the view that if you were going to talk about something you should make an effort to know as much about it as possible. I have rarely felt like the fox who is supposed to know many things. I have been more like a worker bee landing on different flowers. But I have tried to get to know these blooms as well as I could. Some may think the range of this book overambitious, but I hope it reflects this engagement.

Beginning work in a Department of European Studies I have had to do a lot of formal and informal learning on a journey that led me to a hopefully dissident role in a Business School. I have benefited from meeting and sharing workspaces with colleagues and PhD students from a number of countries. A friend who didn't have a passport once said to me that one of the good things about globalization is that it brings the world to you.

I have always had a strong comparative sense. Initially this was focused on eastern Europe, but my interests have spread more widely. I must especially acknowledge the value of meeting with colleagues from China and what I have learned from a number of PhD students from Africa. Having a chance to talk to people and reflect on what they tell you can be illuminating. There are lots of numbers in this book, for example. But I hope too that there is a sense of their limits. If someone who has worked on a street survey in Lagos only to be told that the response rate was not good enough then explains to you how they solved the problem, it opens up questions in your mind not only about the reliability of data but what the perils of its collection tell you about wider social relations.

More narrowly, I must thank Alison Howson, my editor, for thinking of me and advising on the manuscript. Sue Sparks made encouraging comments on a draft and Joseph Haynes used his detailed knowledge of the data and two national statistical offices to offer criticisms and suggestions. Marcie Haynes has patiently answered questions on a wide range of issues as well as coped with my sometimes obsessive interest in some of the weirder aspects of productivity. Needless to say, any mistakes are mine.

# 1

# Productivity: "it is almost everything"

Paul Krugman is one of the world's best-known economists. He has a Nobel Prize in economics and a regular economics column. He once said, "productivity isn't everything, but, in the long run, it is almost everything". Few economists have not heard this quote. The reason productivity is so important, Krugman continued, is that "a country's ability to improve its standard of living over time depends almost entirely on its ability to raise its output per worker" (Krugman 1994a: 11). This makes the idea of productivity look pretty important, and it is. But it has also been suggested that today the word most associated with productivity is *puzzle*. Productivity is a puzzle because it is a problem to understand conceptually; it is a problem to measure; it is a problem to explain and it is a problem to know how to improve it. Much of this book is about this productivity puzzle, but first we need to ask why productivity matters so much.

Imagine that we double the inputs we put into the economy. We might hope to double the output. But getting the same amount out as you put in is not very impressive. It is an example of what is called extensive growth. What we really want is more from the extra bits we put in. We want more output per hectare of land we use, more output per worker and more output per unit of capital. This is called intensive growth. Until the late nineteenth century, economists tended to talk of *productiveness* as a catch-all term. They were not very careful to distinguish between extensive growth and increasing what you get out per unit that is put in. But in the late nineteenth century they began to use the term *productivity* for this second effect. Productivity here is efficiency, it is a ratio of inputs to outputs and it is the driving force of intensive growth.

$$\frac{\text{Output}}{\text{Input}} = \text{Productivity level} \qquad \frac{\text{Changes in outputs}}{\text{Changes in inputs}} = \text{Productivity growth}$$

We can get more out separately from each of the factors of production. There is the land input, and this might lead us to think of *land productivity*. There is labour: the physical and nervous energy we expend. This would lead us to think about *labour productivity*. And there is capital: the buildings, roads, machinery and computers that make our lives easier. This leads to the idea *capital productivity*. Productivity can also refer to getting more out from these factors of production when we combine them: this is what economists mean when they talk of *total factor productivity*.

After 1945 a focus on productivity became central to much of the debate about economic policy and economics. The Cold War seemed to involve a competition of two systems in which victory would go to the one with the superior productivity growth. "History is on our side. We will bury you", said Nikita Khrushchev, the leader of the USSR, in 1956. He was wrong. Just over three and a half decades later the USSR collapsed. But geopolitical tensions have not gone away. China, with its own story of surging productivity growth, has emerged as a new challenger. In the poorer parts of the world, after decolonization, the hope too was to break free of the low-productivity–low-income traps that seemed to characterize the lives of the larger part of the world's population. And in the most advanced regions, governments focused on productivity as one of the most important tests of longer-term economic success as well as one of the keys to shorter-run economic stability. Productivity came to be seen as important to political and social development and cohesion. If productivity growth could increase the size of the cake, there would be more for everyone. The edge would be taken off distributional conflicts.

Before the Second World War, economists had spent a lot of time thinking about distribution. Who gets what and why? The answers raised painful and significant theoretical problems. Economists are usually obsessed with the idea of diminishing returns: the first bit of chocolate you eat is a treat, but if you keep eating it then the pleasure diminishes and you may even become sick. This simple idea leads to an interesting position. An additional pound of income would seem to be more useful to a poor person than a rich one. Taking away a pound from a rich person to redistribute to a poor one looks like a sensible route to improving human welfare. For another Nobel

Prize-winning economist, Robert Lucas, these ideas are steps too far. "Of the tendencies that are harmful to sound economics, the most seductive, and in my opinion the most poisonous, is to focus on questions of distribution", he said in 2004. "The potential for improving the lives of poor people", continued Lucas, "by finding different ways of distributing current production is nothing compared to the apparently limitless potential of increasing production" (Lucas 2004). If in the wider world a "politics of productivity" displaced a "politics of redistribution", so in economics productivity analysis came to loom much larger than the analysis of distribution.

Let us accept this for the moment and look at the idea of "the apparently limitless potential of increasing production". Figure 1.1 shows how output

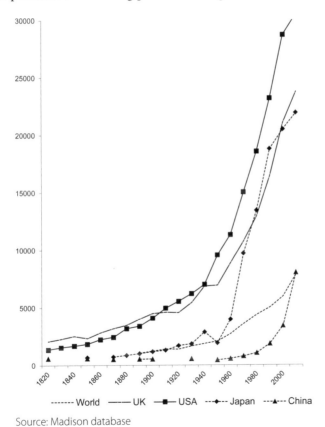

Source: Madison database

**Figure 1.1** Per capita GDP for world and selected countries 1820–2010 in constant $1990

per head has changed globally, and for a number of countries, over nearly 200 years.

Output per head is not as close to a proper productivity measure as we would like. The input is total population – not labour or land and capital. But we do not have to go back too far for our estimates of the size of these inputs to become quite hazy. This figure of output per head will have to serve to illustrate the power of productivity growth. The phrase that is often used to explain how growth works is the "magic of compound interest". Just as money in a bank account earns interest that can then be left there so the next year you get interest on both the original sum and the previous interest, so the same can apply in an economy. Productivity growth builds over time. The higher the rate of growth, the faster the increase in output per head. There is a simple trick that allows us to see this. If the rate of growth is 1 per cent then output per head will double every 70 years. If it is 2 per cent it will take 35 years and 3 per cent only 23.33 years, and so on. The doubling ratio is 70 divided by the rate of growth.

This is what has happened in the advanced world since the late eighteenth century, albeit unevenly. We can see this in the data in Figure 1.1 for the United Kingdom. For a long time, growth seemed restricted to Europe and especially the United States. But more recently some other economies have experienced even faster rates of sustained growth. You can see this in Figure 1.1 in terms of Japan and China. The first surge in output per head in Britain was linked to productivity growth bound up in the industrial revolution. But is the industrial revolution the whole cause of the change? Not quite. For the industrial revolution to work, for it to even be possible, there had to be what Rostow once called "preconditions" (Rostow 1960). These preconditions took a couple of centuries to emerge in western Europe. More radical accounts see the rise of capitalism as central to the development of these preconditions. They also argue that their development often involved major challenges to the old order: revolutions, civil wars and wars. Many mainstream accounts have tried to shut the door firmly against the idea of capitalism. But they then let it in again by the window when they say that to understand the variations in productivity levels and growth, "institutions matter".

Before the advent of capitalism, and especially capitalism in its industrial form, change was painfully slow. People were born, lived and died in societies that seemed to move almost glacially. If the rate of growth was, say, 0.1

per cent, it would take 700 years to double output per head. This makes the creation of new conditions in western Europe from the sixteenth century onwards all the more special. This has also given rise to other major debates. One asks why Europe against, say, China? This is a debate both about when the so-called "great divergence" occurred and why. Relative levels of productivity play a key role in it. A second debate is then about where, when and why in Europe? Here too, arguments about productivity figure prominently. Since our discussion focuses on the modern era we can largely, but not completely, set aside these debates because some elements return when we look at how growth and productivity change has begun to come about in parts of the world that once seemed marginalized in the great divergence.

Figure 1.1 shows that surging growth has continued in some parts of the world. Look at the curves for Japan and then China. The growth in China also helps to explain an important part of the recent growth in global output per head. The bad news is that the gaps in productivity levels across the world are still huge (De Jong 2015). Table 1.1 gives some indicative examples of the gaps today using labour productivity. In this instance it is output – gross domestic product (GDP) – divided by workers rather than population. The measure is still crude but a better indicator than output per head. Because we have these data for a large number of countries, it is perhaps the most used comparative indicator.

**Table 1.1** GDP per person employed in 2018 as percentage of US level

| USA | 100 | Japan | 63 | China | 27 |
|---|---|---|---|---|---|
| France | 74 | South Korea | 61 | India | 15 |
| Germany | 73 | Russian Fed. | 45 | Nigeria | 13 |
| UK | 70 | South Africa | 36 | Niger | 2 |

*Source*: US Conference Board.

Where productivity has grown the most, real wages have risen and the prices of goods fallen in relative terms, so that even those on average incomes enjoy standards of living once only available to monarchs and their richest supporters. The great economist Joseph Schumpeter, who we will encounter at a number of points, put this well, even if in the slightly misogynistic terms of his day,

> Queen Elizabeth [the First] owned silk stockings. The capital-
> ist achievement does not typically consist in providing more silk
> stockings for queens but in bringing them within the reach of
> factory girls in return for steadily decreasing amounts of effort.
>
> (Schumpeter 1976 [1943]: 67)

To see the effect of this we only have to look at the amount of goods that we, in the advanced world, have and take for granted.

One type of productivity growth, more than any other, has made this possible. This is agricultural productivity. Agriculture once dominated human life because its productivity was so low. Peasants had to put almost all their effort into growing food. They got barely enough out to feed themselves, their lords and the small urban population. Yet in the last two centuries agricultural productivity has risen to such an extent that the word's population has grown from 1 billion in 1800 to some 8 billion today. More impressive, we also eat better. If we do not it is not because there is not enough food but because some of the world's population (ironically mostly in the countryside) lack the means to access it – the distribution issue again. Giovanni Federico has estimated that in the years 1800–70 the global food supply more or less expanded at the same rate as the population. This refuted the pessimism of Thomas Malthus who thought that population would always grow faster than the food supply. Then, in the decades 1870–1938, the global food supply may have increased at 0.15 per cent per head and, after 1945, at 0.56 per cent per head. Since 1945 it seems that agricultural productivity has grown everywhere, albeit to different degrees. What this has meant is that although the global population rose six to seven times between 1800 and 2000, the food supply increased around ten times (Federico 2005: 20).

We can see agricultural revolutions happening along with industrialization from the late eighteenth century in the advanced world. But Federico's figures reflect the ways in which the really big global revolution has come about since 1945 in the poor world, and not least with new hybrid crops. Rising agricultural productivity means that fewer workers have been needed to produce the same or more. In 1800 some 80 per cent of the global labour force worked the land in one way or another. As late as 1950 it was still around two-thirds, but today it is down to some 30 per cent. The share has not only fallen relatively, but in the 2000s it even began to fall absolutely as productivity rose. The share, of course, varies enormously. In Africa, a farmer may today produce enough to feed several others. In Germany and the US, a farmer is said to supply 160 others (Handelsbatt Research Institute 2017: 10). Other forms of productivity growth will loom large in this book and perhaps seem more spectacular than the changes in agricultural productivity, but they are only possible because, when it comes to the food supply, we can now get so much more out from what we put in.

As agricultural productivity has grown, we have been able to move from working on the farm to working in urban factories and offices. In 1800 around 2 per cent of the world's population lived in towns and cities. The figure was 8 per cent in 1900, 46 per cent in 2000 and over 50 per cent in 2019. Urban life has a host of problems – the world has been described as "a planet of slums" – but even for the poorest, the push of problems in the countryside is probably second to the pull of their "cities of dreams" (Davis 2006).

Life expectancy, too, has risen as productivity has grown. People have become healthier, grown taller and, in recent times, heavier and wider. Productivity growth has enabled us to develop the social infrastructures necessary for healthy lives. When we think of gains we normally think of machines, not sewers or running water. But where such systems do not exist, dealing with excrement and getting fresh water is fraught with difficulties. A bad sanitary situation weakens us with disease; it leads to high death rates, especially for infants and children, and low productivity. A good sanitary situation is part of a virtuous circle of productivity growth.

Higher productivity also gives us more time for things other than work. When productivity is low people will have to spend their lives working, even if at lower levels of work intensity. When productivity grows, we can devote more of our years to full-time education at its start and retirement at its end. And during the "productive period" we will spend fewer hours in labour each year, creating the potential for more "leisure". We shop, we go to concerts, we are entertained. All of these achievements are made possible by increased productivity: our ability to do more with the resources we have.

Capturing all this in a single productivity measure is not possible. Economists usually focus on the narrowly economic and assume that if they add up output then they have a good enough measure of our welfare or well-being. One number above all reflects this, that of GDP. It has been said to be "the most powerful statistical figure in human history" (Lepenies 2016: ix). GDP data have only been systematically collected since 1945. Today it, and the various elements that make up GDP, are the most commonly used measures of inputs and outputs. At the level of national economies GDP is more often than not the numerator that we want to divide by the denominator to get our productivity measures. Is it enough? If we think of well-being in a wider sense it is possible to imagine many other ways of measuring productivity gains.

The Human Development Index combines income per head, life expectancy and education. This simplifies the issues but produces fewer interesting results since these components seem to be closely related over time. Other indices stretch more widely, extending even to try to measure the happiness of people on the planet. These composite indicators encounter similar problems. Which indicators do we include? How do we measure them? How do we combine them into a single index (a weighting problem)? How do we scale them? (A GDP indicator is unlimited; many other indicators are often scaled at 1–100.) The Organisation for Economic Co-operation and Development (OECD) "Better Life Initiative", which began to be published in 2011, is especially interesting here. This not only tries to build a set of comprehensive indicators across countries but it has also been the basis of an attempt to push these indicators back to 1820. Its breadth multiplies the problems. Nevertheless, it is worth illustrating the complexity of the links between productivity change and other indicators by looking at what their historical data show (OECD 2014).

Some components seem strongly positively correlated to GDP per head, using this as a crude productivity indicator. These include life expectancy, health indicators and education, although the closeness of the correlation has weakened in recent decades. Other components are positively, but more loosely, correlated, such as the indicators of "political integration", "personal security" and gender equality. One group of indicators has a strong negative correlation: the environmental ones and not least those relating to biodiversity and pollution. Another indicator – income inequality – seems to increase early on in development and then falls, although what has been happening recently is more controversial.

This suggests that if productivity growth has the potential to improve things, it does not always deliver on this promise. In fact, in the shorter run the connections of productivity and the growth of human welfare seem looser still. In the early industrial revolution in Britain, for example, productivity growth does not seem to have been reflected in similar increases in real wages, life expectancy, height indicators, etc. The benefits of productivity change were captured more by capital than labour, by the rich rather than the masses. The economic historian R. C. Allen has called this an "Engels pause" after Marx's collaborator, Frederick Engels, who described the poverty of the Manchester working class in his 1845 *Condition of the Working Class in England*. This is far from being just of historical interest. If people at the start of the nineteenth century lived through a big productivity disconnect, we may be experiencing the same disconnect at the start of the twenty-first century. A big gap seems to have opened up again between productivity growth and the distribution of any gains, possibly creating a new Engels pause (Allen 2011, 2017).

Clearly even within a narrow analysis of productivity there is a lot going on that needs to be explored, but is a narrow analysis of productivity adequate?

## Productivity and the bigger picture

Economic journals are full of productivity discussions but many of them seem weird. There is, for example, a literature on the productivity of the tobacco industry, past and present, in which the outputs are the numbers and or values of cigarettes and cigars and the inputs are land, labour and capital. Such calculations are even used to explore the "highest productivity" examples of producing cigarettes to encourage emulation. The story of how tobacco came to be and still is produced on a commercial scale tends not figure, nor do the conditions of production in the tobacco factories. Still less does that fact that one of the outputs of the industry is death. Some studies now suggest that two in three smokers will die prematurely from some smoking-related disease. This might seem an extreme example but it is not. Economists who discuss productivity often put on blinkers which prevent them seeing the strangeness of what they are doing. They ignore the way that productivity growth takes place within a larger system and the question of how are we to define that system. This makes productivity growth seem bigger than it is, it makes it seem less contradictory and less conflictual. As we shall see as this book proceeds, there are many narrow productivity puzzles to address, but we need to start with these big ones.

First let's think about what the system is whose productivity we are analysing. The answer is that the real system is the planet on which we live, a "finite, non-expanding, materially closed" world (Daly & Kunkel 2018: 88). Most economists have tended to baulk at the implications of defining the system this way. They prefer to isolate some narrowly defined "economy" and, within it, some narrow productivity measures, and analyse or deal with the bigger issues in an ad hoc way. Not all have done so. Even within conventional economic thinking, some pioneers like Nicholas Georgescu-Roegen, Kenneth Boulding and Herman Daly thought about the economy as being part of a total system. Once seen as marginal, they are now considered more significant, not least as we see the links between the economy and ecological crisis. Figure 1.2 is a rather crude expression of the basic arguments of Georgescu-Roegen, one of the many major economists never awarded a Nobel Prize. Simple though it is, it forces us to ask questions about where inputs come from, not least the raw materials and the labour. It suggests that you cannot assume that they exist or treat them as a free good. It also points to the fact that any activity in the system will have multiple outputs and effects, some desired and others undesired. The undesired examples most obvious in our minds today are pollution and global warming, but undesired effects are as many and numerous as desired ones. It also points to the ways in which productivity growth can have multiple causes, multiple effects and multiple forms of feedback. Productivity change, we shall argue, is a dynamic process in which questions of stability and sustainability are crucial.

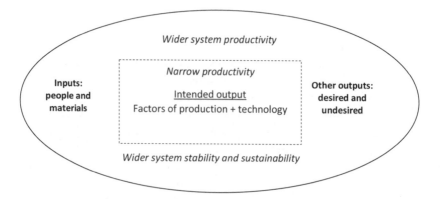

**Figure 1.2** The economy as part of a larger closed system

Thinking of the system as the planet makes sense in terms of dealing with something like global warming where its causes can occur anywhere and its effects go everywhere. But can we not isolate a narrower productivity change within, say, a national economy? In the abstract we can measure the productivity of anything: a field, a machine, an hour or a lifetime of labour, a company, a regional or national economy. But because capitalism exists as a world of competing states, and because it is states that do most of the measuring, then our attention tends to be drawn to *national* economic units. Yet we know that economic processes continually pass over or through the barriers that states try to create to contain them. We will look in Chapter 3 at some of the technical problems this creates for productivity measurement, but here our interest is more a logical one. If there is a global economy, what sense does it make to slice and dice the economic process geographically and to consider productivity gains in country A without also paying attention to their possible relations to countries or areas B and C?

The foundations for modern productivity growth began to be laid in Europe from the sixteenth century onwards. The process was helped by a flow of goods – precious metals, foodstuffs and raw materials – from the Americas. But what would happen to our analysis of productivity if we accounted for the geographical totality of this? In the sixteenth century the Americas saw a catastrophic population loss as the native population was wiped out by disease and exploitation. We know too that the local population was replaced by a more "productive" (that word again) slave workforce torn from their families in Africa, and that the slave trade lasted well into the nineteenth century. Should not any attempt to calculate productivity of the parts of this bigger system also be guided by a sense of looking at the whole? This is a problem that does not go away. Capitalism has always been a complex global system, but the level of complexity has grown in recent decades as deeper global supply chains have been created.

> World production is now structured into global value chains in which firms source parts, components and services from producers in several countries and in turn sell their output to firms and consumers worldwide. The typical "Made in" labels in manufactured goods have become archaic symbols of an old era. Today, most goods are "Made in the World".
>
> (World Trade Organization 2018: v)

We marvel at what we can do with our smartphones. We know vaguely that iPhones are assembled in China with machines and cheap labour, but we are less aware of where the many parts come from or how they are produced. One of the crucial raw materials, for example, is the rare metal tantalum or coltan. Some of this is dug out of the ground in failing states in Africa by artisanal miners using their hand tools while they are watched over by men with guns. Yet when economists talk of the complexity of measuring the productivity impact of digital technologies, they tend not to mean an analysis of the global value chain and a consideration of aspects like this.

*What* is the system and *where* is it seem obvious, but there is also a *when* question. The effects of productivity growth can also extend into the future, so "time" should be a factor in any analysis of productivity. "In the long run", Keynes said, "we are all dead". But those who come after will hopefully be very much alive, so this does not really solve the problem of "future effects", be they good or ill. Economists long ago realized that adding time to an economic model was an interesting logical issue, not least for the idea of "perfect" markets. But in recent decades we have come to realize that it is also a pressing practical problem: the future matters. At the level of theory this is often discussed as the problem of intergenerational (or intertemporal) efficiency and intergenerational justice (see Solow 1986).

A minority of economists solve the problem of time by arguing that we have no duty to the future. They believe that we can place trust in the future having the resources and technology to deal with any problems we create today. It is possible that through productivity growth today we might create more wealth and opportunities for ourselves and for those who come later. In the rich world, we have partly been beneficiaries of this positive link. Another possibility is that we could seek to ensure that those in the future are as well off as we are; a version of this "rule" was proposed in the 1970s by John Hartwick. The third possibility is that we might maximize our well-being today at the expense of that in the future. In fact, a good case can be made that this is what is now happening, with the consequence that "our" apparent productivity gains may be being obtained at the expense of constraints in the future. The productivity growth associated with industrialization, for example, has come about on the basis of the increasing exhaustion of natural resources: minerals and fossil fuels. Such productivity gains can be argued to have been a product of the reckless exploitation of an opportunity only available once for humanity. No less the outputs we create can also have extended legacy effects, both positive and negative. Nuclear energy, for example, produces spent fuel that can remain dangerous for generations to come. Only the smaller part of it is recycled. The larger part is stored in the hope that future generations will look after it or will find a solution regarding what to do with it. But how do we adequately factor this into a calculation of the productivity of the nuclear fuel industry, or the energy industry and the economy more widely?

## The problem of goods and bads

Everything we do has multiple effects, some good, some bad. Orthodox economists struggle to deal with this. They tend to analyse economic relations as if all the costs and all the gains can be priced and then focused in the transactions between the individuals directly involved: you sell, I buy. We can therefore measure:

$$\frac{\text{private gain}}{\text{private cost}}$$

Where the private gain exceeds the private cost, a thing is worth doing and the thing that is worth doing most of all is that which produces the biggest gain for the least cost.

Economists recognize that this does not work well for what are called "public goods", where the market prices do not fully capture the gains. They also recognize that when economic activity occurs there are other effects. But these are usually dealt with, at least at the elementary level, by the assumption of *ceteris paribus* or "taking all other things as being equal". Using rather more sophisticated techniques we can try to extend this analysis to look more widely at social rates of return where other effects are considered. We then have:

$$\frac{\text{social gains}}{\text{social costs}}$$

When we try to broaden our analysis to consider what might go into this bigger calculation, we can distinguish two kind of effects. There are *complementarities* that affect the direct parties to the transaction and there are *externalities* which affect third parties. Complementarities and externalities can be both positive and negative. If I "choose" to smoke for pleasure and this kills me then my death is a negative complementarity of my transaction with the tobacco supplier. If my smoking leads to another person dying of passive smoking then this would be a negative externality.

If the market does not capture these effects properly, economists talk of market failure. In the past, economists have tended to proceed as if, both in theory and practice, these effects were not very serious. Enlightened governments could maintain the market system but adjust it through modest taxes, subsidies, regulations or even by creating pseudo markets in pollutants to make prices more fully reflect real costs. In practice, these multiple effects are intrinsic to all economic activity, and they are serious. Global warming, for example, has been called by Nicholas Stern the "*biggest* market failure the world has seen" (Stern 2008: 1).

The problem is to find a way of systematically addressing these multiple effects in economic analysis in general and productivity analysis in particular. Even the way economists separate out these effects is a problem. Herman Daly, for example, has said that, "we classify as 'external' costs for no better reason than because we have made no provision for them in our economic theories" (Daly & Kunkel 2018). The same can be said to apply to complementarities. Smokers like to think that the main effect of smoking is pleasure and their own and other peoples' deaths are unfortunate side effects, but they are both effects. This kind of labelling is an act of self-deception at the level of the individual; at the level of society it is an ideological trick. Drug companies do this when they treat the effects they want as "good" and the effects they don't want as "side" effects. Viagra seems to have multiple effects, but it is marketed according to the one that puts it in the best light. Economists play the same trick all the time, not least when looking at productivity analysis. You might come to feel as you read this book that economists' discovery of productivity as the basis of economic virility rather makes it the Viagra of economics.

To calculate productivity, we need some way of measuring the cost of inputs and the value of outputs based on a common denominator. But the only one we have is price. This is fine if everything has a price and there is a price for everything. But is there? In cigarette smoking how do we price the different complementarities and the externalities, especially the deaths and the ill-health? Some economists think the answer is simple: we estimate a price for them. In this instance there is a huge literature on health economics that tries to deal with this. We will not go there. Our interest here is to draw attention to the logical problem. This problem is not peculiar to our example of cigarettes; it appears everywhere, not least in the analysis of the impact of ecological problems. What price can we put on global warming?

Unfortunately, this is only half the problem. Suppose we can price these things: how does this affect, say, our measurement of output in a productivity measure? Look at the two ways of calculating productivity below:

$$= \frac{\text{good outputs} - \text{bad outputs}}{\text{inputs}} = \frac{\text{good outputs} + \text{bad outputs}}{\text{inputs}}$$

The first looks sensible but the second is actually what economists often do. The rules of national income accounting – which, as we shall see in Chapter 3, give us much of the data that go into productivity analysis – say that total output is the sum of the market or estimated market values of what is done. Some of the key individuals who helped create the basis of national income accounting thought a wrong road was being taken. Not everything that earns an income actually contributes to real output. Their arguments were dismissed, and although they are again beginning to be taken more seriously, the old idea still rules. A disaster can add to national income because the costs of cleaning up to get back to where you were also add to national income. In a road accident the costs of repair and the health costs of putting you and other victims back together add to the output part of any calculation of national productivity. Crime might be bad but just think about the way that trying to prevent it and dealing with it adds to national income. Every economic student learns about this paradox in the elementary discussions of how we measure output. But, as with the issues of complementarities and externalities, there has been a growing awareness that the scale of this problem has been too easily passed over. This has in no small way contributed to an undermining of the credibility of national income measures as output indicators, including in productivity analysis.

The productivity miracle of the modern dairy cow illustrates the need to look at both the good outputs and the literal excrement ones (Box 1.1).

15

## BOX 1.1. PRODUCTIVITY ANALYSIS AND THE MODERN DAIRY COW

A modern dairy cow seems to be a miracle of productivity growth. Figure 1.3 shows the milk yield for cows in the UK. In 1860s Britain the average cow gave about seven pints of milk a day. By the late 1940s this had risen to ten pints a day. But in 2015 it was an astonishing 34 pints of milk a day from a single cow. And that is just an average.

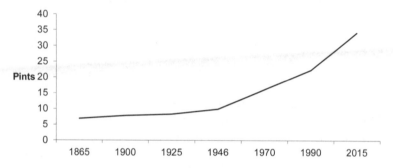

**Figure 1.3** Average pints per day from UK dairy cow, 1865–2015

Milk yield is the crudest of productivity indicators and no economist would be satisfied with this. They would certainly want to look a little deeper at the inputs of land, labour and capital and they would want to think about the value of the milk output. But there are other things. To achieve such yields cows have been specially bred by artificial insemination. They are bigger, heavier and less mobile than ever before. They are often kept in conditions we prefer not to look at. They have to be fed and this involves not just grass but soya-based animal feeds. Soya is grown on land that was once forested, adding to global warming. Cows are pumped with antibiotics and growth hormones. Milk and its products are not the only output. Cows contribute to global warming by their methane-producing belching and flatulence. Not very nice but a very real effect. The more food that goes into the front of our cow, the more (sorry to be crude again, but this is real life) that comes out of the back (approximately 12 to 15 times a day if you ask). In fact, in weight terms a dairy cow will probably produce more urine and manure than milk – in the UK that is enough for the dairy herd to fill Wembley Stadium up to the roof several times over each year. This is causing a massive headache. In Holland, the government is even paying some farmers to send their dairy cows to slaughter because there is no more room for the extra waste they produce. Some of the antibiotics and hormones also come out again in the animal products and the manure, from where they can leech into the water supply. So, we have three very different ways of looking at productivity. There is a technical story about milk yield. There is a narrow economic story that looks at the value of milk outputs and the immediate costs of the inputs. And there is, potentially at least, a broad, "holistic" story that tries to include all effects: wanted and unwanted. The question is, which story do we want to tell?

---

## Productivity: an end or a means?

Should productivity be our goal? It has been said that "productivity is for robots". Humans are not machines, not a means whose use is determined by the economic system. Too many economists imagine that ends come from outside the economic system. Yet it has been a central part of the critique of capitalism for nearly 200 years that "ends" are imposed on us. Instead of being "for" something, productivity has tended to become an end in itself or a reflection of ends that we cannot control. Marx called this alienation. The economic system we create, rules and controls us. The result is that we seem to live on a productivity treadmill. We are made to tread ever harder to keep the motion going. A century ago R. H. Tawney wrote that when people:

> desire to place their economic life on a better foundation, they repeat, like parrots, the word "Productivity," because that is the word that rises first in their minds; regardless of the fact that productivity is the foundation on which it is based already, that increased productivity is the one characteristic achievement of the age ... as religion was of the Middle Ages or art of classical Athens, and that it is precisely in the century which has seen the greatest increase in productivity since the fall of the Roman Empire that economic discontent has been most acute. (Tawney 1921: 4–5)

When Tawney wrote, the productivity obsession was just starting. Today it is part of our lives. We are involved in productivity races, and are part of productivity drives. Our lives are divided into productive and unproductive parts. Work is done under pressure. We live in what have been called "prisons of measured time". We are told to use time productively, to be careful how we spend it, to get the best out of it and so on. We are obsessed with our own "performance" and that of the institutions that surround us. We are even encouraged to measure, record, count and compare the most basic elements of what we do. At work we are not asked to "reason why". Then, as consumers, we "are persuaded to spend money we don't have, on things we don't need, to create impressions that won't last, on people we don't care about" (Tim Jackson quoted in Raworth 2018: 113). The relentless focus on the "productivity" of everything does not seem to be a good system, and it produces a whole range of problems for us and the world we inhabit.

Does productivity even make us happy, either as individuals or a species? If our output measure is our welfare then its subjective as well as objective components are important. Philosophers have always recognized this. Economists less so. However, some have become interested in trying to measure happiness and life satisfaction as an outcome. Richard Easterlin was one of the pioneers of this. His original analysis suggested that happiness rises with income, but only to a point. Beyond that point the "Easterlin paradox" sets in: additions to output do not necessarily produce a greater sense of well-being. Some dismiss this result as an artefact of the measures, some dismiss it on data grounds, but others have replicated and explored it (Easterlin 1974; Layard 2011; Coyle 2015).

If such a gap exists it further undermines the idea that productivity growth is a good means to achieve greater welfare and life satisfaction. Not only might there be no link for high-income societies but it might even be the case that by keeping pressure on the productivity accelerator, we might actually be decreasing welfare in our work and non-work lives. In the abstract both policy-makers and economists are happy to recognize this. We live the paradox in our daily lives too. Yet the pressure of competition is such that any attempt to try to ease the pressure is met with bewilderment for its lack of "realism".

## Productivity and distribution

It is now time to return to the issue that Robert Lucas advised against giving too much attention to: distribution. There are two aspects to the distribution question. One is about the size of factor shares. This refers to the way that the value created in an economy appears to reward land as rent, capital as profit and labour as wages. The classical economist David Ricardo wrote that, "to determine the laws which regulate this *distribution*, is the principal problem in Political Economy" (Atkinson 2009: 4). The second is the distribution of incomes (and wealth) to individuals (and organizations). The two are related because at the top the ownership of capital means access to profits, but to illustrate the problems we will focus on the personal distribution of income.

The optimistic view is captured in the idea of a Kuznets curve – named after Simon Kuznets, one of the pioneers of economic measurement. In the 1950s Kuznets hypothesized (he had little evidence) that when productivity growth begins to develop the level of inequality initially rises but then falls, reduced by natural economic forces and government policy. The inequality curve would have an inverted U shape as in Figure 1.4.

Kuznets was always the first to recognize the limits of his data. Unlike Lucas, he was positive towards ideas of redistribution. He also warned against "the fatally simple remedy of an authoritarian regime, [using] the popu-lation as cannon-fodder in the fight for economic achievement" (Kuznets 1955: 25). But these were not the conclusions that most drew. Some argued that the U-shaped curve was support for the idea that a growth in inequality, especially early on, was necessary, even good for productivity and growth. Others comforted themselves with the idea that beyond a certain point ine-quality would naturally diminish.

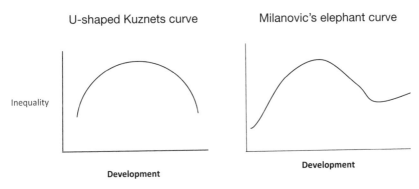

**Figure 1.4** Hypotheses about economic development and the level of inequality

Today neither argument looks persuasive. Equalizing tendencies seemed to have been reversed in a number of countries and global regions (Piketty 2014). The rewards of productivity growth look to be skewed again more towards the few than the many (remember the Engels pause?). Much effort is now being put into tracking long-run trends in income and wealth inequality to set the more recent ones in this bigger context, as well as trying to explain the resulting patterns. Instead of the optimistic stylized U-shaped Kuznets curve we now have an alternative and more pessimistic stylized alternative: the elephant curve proposed by Branko Milanovic. Here we see that the rewards of later productivity growth also seem to be being captured more by some than others (Milanovic 2016).

There is another debate about distribution and productivity increases. How are the rewards for productivity growth distributed along global supply or value chains? The different geographical parts are said to generate and get different amounts of value. The question is, do the different parts get rewards proportionate to what they put in? Critics argue that rewards flow more to some parts of the chain than others. These tend to be the parts located in rich countries. If producers in poor countries get trapped in the lower-value parts of the chain then these chains begin to look more like "poverty chains" for them (Selwyn 2018). This is not to say that productivity growth has no positive impact in some poorer countries. We shall show later that it has significantly improved the lives of part of the world's poor in a way that was not thought possible 50 years ago. But this does not stop us asking the question about whether the overall distribution has still been unequal.

We also need to ask questions about how the bad side of productivity growth is distributed. Here there is less argument. Within countries, the reason that rich folks tend to "live on the hill" is not only because of the view but because it is cleaner and safer up there. The bad stuff, both metaphorically and in practice, tends to flow downhill. The same is true across countries. Rich countries make the biggest demands on the system. They have even seemingly improved their environmental record by outsourcing part of the downside of dirty productivity growth to the developing world. Unfortunately, the governments and populations in these countries have fewer means to deal with the consequences.

There is a final big issue we wish to raise about productivity and distribution. If we view productivity dynamically then distribution issues will feed back. So, is inequality good or bad for future productivity growth?

Conventional economists stress the value of unequal rewards as incentives. They argue that efficiency losses arise from attempts at redistribution. The counter-argument is that productivity growth depends more on cooperation and trust than individualistic competition. Far from unequal societies having higher productivity growth, they might well have lower levels of productivity growth. At one level this might be an argument about theoretical systems: "capitalism" versus "socialism", for example. But it is also an argument about variation within systems and not least capitalism as it exists. This is sometimes called the varieties of capitalism debate. Does a less equal or a more equal "capitalism" perform better? Answering this question is not easy because so many things can affect productivity. But the interesting thing is that the tests that have been done and which seem robust tend to support the argument that, in narrow economic terms, more equal societies perform better than less equal ones. If we widen the debate to consider more social variables, then the evidence in favour of the equality argument seems to become even more compelling (Alesina & Rodrik 1994; Rodrik 2007).

But now we need to dig deeper. In Chapter 2 we shall try to set out some of the answers to the question of how productivity grows. Chapter 3 looks at the intensifying debate on productivity measurement. In Chapter 4 we ask if productivity can go on forever. Chapter 5 looks at productivity in the advanced world. Chapter 6 looks at the productivity stories of the Asian Tigers and China. In Chapter 7 we look at Africa's productivity failure. In Chapter 8, the final chapter, now with a stronger sense of the problems we face, we return to these big issues.

# 2
# How does productivity happen?

We have seen that productivity is a ratio. The numerator is some measure of output, the denominator is some measure of input. There are physical productivity measures. We can calculate the tonnage of wheat grown per hectare; we can count the number of cars produced per worker; we could calculate the number of examination passes per 100 students. Leave aside whether this would capture or explain everything we are interested in. These physical measures of productivity can only take us so far. Economists are more interested in inputs as a cost and outputs as value. This potentially gives us the three different types of productivity measure, as set out in Figure 2.1.

If we take land productivity, we can still have a single-input measure that divides the monetary value of output by a physical input or a value input. In agriculture the value of agricultural output per unit of land input is an example. We can also look at labour productivity in terms of the value of output per person (effectively an output per head calculation), per worker or, best of all if the data are available, per hour worked. These measures are some of the most basic and widely used measures of productivity. When it comes to the productivity of capital things are different. We cannot add up a plough, a hammer and a computer. We can only measure the value of output against the value of the capital used. To measure the value of output against all inputs too, we need prices. We cannot add hectares of land to numbers of

| $\dfrac{\text{Physical output}}{\text{Physical input}}$ | $\dfrac{\text{Value output}}{\text{Physical input}}$ | $\dfrac{\text{Value output}}{\text{Value input}}$ |
|---|---|---|
| Example: Agricultural yield, miles per gallon | Value output per worker/per hour | Value output per wage unit |

**Figure 2.1** Three types of productivity measure

workers and machines as inputs. And we cannot add the weight of wheat to the number of cars or the meals cooked as outputs. We have no choice but to add up the cost of the inputs and the value of outputs.

Table 2.1 sets out the basic productivity measures that economists use following this logic (OECD 2001).

**Table 2.1** The economist's basic measures

| Output measure | Value gross output/value added | | | | |
|---|---|---|---|---|---|
| Input measure | Single-factor inputs | | | Combined inputs | |
| | Land | Labour | Capital | 1+2+3 | Technical change |
| | Land productivity | Labour productivity | Capital productivity | Multi-factor productivity | The residual |

Notice that there is an additional element shown in Table 2.1. This is the idea of an unknown component, or "knowledge" component, embodied in the changing technology of doing things. We increase output by adding more land, labour and capital. But we also increase it by better using our inputs and using them differently as our "knowledge" grows. This additional element is the crucial bit of any long-term sustained growth in productivity. We can write this out as what economists call a production function:

Land + Labour + Capital + "Technology" = Output

Productivity accounting is an attempt to measure the changing size of the contributions of land, labour, capital and the knowledge element to any changes in additions to output (Solow 1956):

$$\frac{\text{change in outputs}}{\text{change in factor inputs}} + \text{"technical progress"} = \text{productivity growth}$$

Such calculations claim to show that a certain amount of output change can be explained by increases in inputs, and a certain amount by the knowledge

**Table 2.2** Estimated contribution of sources of growth

| | World | | Mature economies | | Emerging economies | |
|---|---|---|---|---|---|---|
| | 2000–7 | 2010–17 | 2000–7 | 2010–17 | 2000–7 | 2010–17 |
| GDP | 4.3 | 3.5 | 2.9 | 2.1 | 6.1 | 4.3 |
| Labour input | 0.9 | 0.8 | 0.7 | 0.7 | 1.3 | 0.9 |
| Capital input | 2.4 | 2.5 | 1.7 | 1.1 | 3.3 | 3.9 |
| Total factor productivity | 1.0 | 0.1 | 0.5 | 0.2 | 1.6 | 0.0 |

*Source*: US Conference Board.

or what is sometimes called the unknown "x" factor. We can then com-pare the balance over time and between countries. Table 2.2 shows a typi-cal example of the results we might get from such productivity accounting (allowing for rounding).

In Chapter 3 we shall look at some of the problems of productivity accounting. The important thing here is that even if we can trust what is done, knowing that, say, 30 per cent of productivity growth is explained by increases in capital and labour and 70 per cent by "knowledge" in country A, but the ratio is 40:60 in country B, doesn't advance our understanding very much.

The real problem is knowing how things interact: the whys and hows of productivity growth. Economists' discussions here often seem to involve a huge theoretical and empirical black box. Inputs go into the black box. Outputs emerge from the other end. What happens inside remains hidden. Over time economists have tried to make their analysis more sophisticated, less by opening up the black box than pulling hidden elements into the light and trying to measure more input effects and more output effects. This is really no different from looking at the ingredients and food values on the packet of a ready meal and thinking you understand how the meal has been made. The (chemical) ingredients on the packaging and the meal on your plate tell you nothing about the bits in between: the food culture, the structure of agribusiness, eating habits, how the ingredients were brought together, food preparation, cooking styles and methods, different people's diets, etc. The real study of productivity change is an applied subject in which there is much to learn from the real businesses and those who study them and not just from testing models or hypotheses against big data sets.

The restrictiveness of much economic thinking about productivity can be seen in its narrow view of "technical change". We can think about technical change in terms of the creation and design of new or better products and the mechanization of their production. But technical change is a broader process. We can find new raw materials and ways of extracting, creating and using them more efficiently. We can create better and new forms of organization, institutions and so on. Behind any change in "technique" will also be an advance in human knowledge. (Possibly, in the future, we may have to add machine knowledge given the advances in artificial intelligence.) This new knowledge can be codified and written down in patents, instruction manuals, even textbooks. But it can involve *tacit* elements of learned skills. There is a difference between having a recipe book and being able to cook a decent meal from it. We learn by doing. This is not a trivial point. One of the big problems in the effective transmission of knowledge to improve productivity is often the lack of tacit skills. This is apparent within advanced economies but it is even more apparent when they are compared to less advanced ones. The lack of tacit skills helps to explain why advanced equipment, when sent to poorer countries, is often less productive, underutilized and even broken.

## From specialization to new methods

How then might productivity grow? One part of the answer was given by Adam Smith in his *Wealth of Nations* in 1776. This is specialization and the division of labour. Smith used the example of a pin factory. An untrained worker, trying to make a whole pin, he said, would struggle to make 20 a day. But Smith had visited a pin factory where ten workers specializing in the different parts of pin production together produced 48,000 pins a day. On average they each produced 4,800 pins a day, a pretty impressive productivity increase (Smith 1970 [1776]: 109–10). We don't know if he really saw this, but we do know that specialization enables time to be saved. The pin workers also got better and more skilled at what they were doing, so this specialized division of labour boosted output per worker. The existence of a pin factory itself – a unit doing one thing – is also an example of specialization. Some of us will work the land, some work in pin factories, still others as teachers in schools and so on. Smith argued that the bigger the market the greater the specialization possible. As the units in which we work increase in size there will also be additional productivity gains from economies of scale in production, organization, buying and selling. Firms doing similar things will tend to cluster together too. Supporting networks will develop that can boost productivity. A degree of specialization by area had long existed when Smith wrote, but it intensified with industrialization. By the end of the nineteenth century the economist Alfred Marshall was talking of the role of these areas as "industrial districts". Manchester was "Cottonopolis": a city not just of the mills making cloth but home to many of the processes that went with it. Today economists talk of the efficiencies that come from specialization by area as agglomeration economies. (But don't forget Chapter 1: there will also be agglomeration diseconomies.) The things we get from China actually come from specific places. Like Manchester, some have informal names too – we can find a Chinese "jean town", a "bra town", even "a toilet town" – reflecting the continuing role of agglomeration economies. And they remain important in the advanced countries, although their forms have changed. The attention that Manchester once got has in recent decades been given to "Silicon Valley". Even in the service sector things cluster to benefit from agglomeration economies. There have long been financial districts, but as finance has grown in importance these districts have grown outwards and, it seems, ever upwards.

Productivity gains related to specialization and the division of labour can only take us so far. Bigger gains come from changing the process of production by finding new ways of doing things, including developing better tools and equipment. Agricultural productivity increased, for example, when the sickle was replaced by the scythe. It increased more (although uncertainly because they did not always work well) when mechanical reapers were introduced. Today a modern combine harvester takes only a few hours to bring in a huge harvest and bale the hay. It leaves nothing behind save for the birds. Adam Smith's pin manufactory disappeared too as pins came to be produced by automated machines that now churn out hundreds of thousands of pins a day.

Where does technical change come from? It seems an obvious question yet many economic models treat it as a gift, something that is exogenous to the system. The phrase sometimes used is, "manna from heaven". But if technological change is not something which exists outside of the economic system (go back to the question we posed in Chapter 1) then it seems unwise to treat it, and by extension other productivity-enhancing elements, as a something freely available to all. One seeming solution to this is what is called "endogenous growth theory". Here research and development, and "human capital" in the form of education, are seen as input variables that can be manipulated (usually by governments) to increase the growth of productivity (Romer 1994). But the focus in endogenous growth theory is still on better manipulating the ingredients rather than understanding how processes and institutions affect inputs and outputs and their interactions.

### The embodiment problem

There is another problem. Even at the level of a single factor, the amount of output we get from a hectare of land or an hour of labour depends upon how land and labour interact with each other and, crucially, how they interact with capital. The more and better the capital we have, the more we can produce. But much economic discussion of productivity change assumes that somehow technological and wider organizational change is *disembodied*. This means that the effects of adding inputs can be separated from the better ways of using them. This is part of the logic of the productivity accounting already set out in Figure 2.2 (Solow 1956).

The idea that technical change can be separated out from the role of increases in capital stocks seems strange, not least in an economy that we define as *capital*ist. When technological change occurs, some machines, buildings, etc. will become obsolete and completely lose their value. Some bits will struggle on, perhaps supported by cheap labour. Still other bits may be improved by modification. But technological change will also need new machines, new plants, new offices, new infrastructures, etc. This requires sustained and, in some instances, increased capital accumulation. This *embodiment* process also means that in analysing investment and the stock of capital, the age of the parts (or its vintage) becomes important. As Hahn and Matthews put it when this problem was beginning to be worked through, "the manna of technical progress falls on the latest machines" (Hahn & Matthews 1965: 60). Sadly the age or vintage of the capital stock is very difficult to measure.

This problem of embodiment also appears when we look at labour. The labour input is partly about quantity and partly about quality. In recent decades more and more attention has been given to this quality issue. Education is the big example. Still, a more educated worker will only be a more productive worker if they have the equipment that allows them to "capitalize" (note that word) on their education. Educating people to read will not be helpful unless they have books to read and, where necessary, the light to read them by. Teaching people to program computers will not be of much value if there are no computers and no electricity to power them.

So, treating inputs as if they can be varied independently of one another is a big issue. Sadly, many economic accounts of productivity change prefer to assume that productivity change is disembodied. It seems easier to think in these terms even though this may be another example of the approach of the drunk who looks for lost keys under the street lamp because that is where the light is.

## Static and dynamic productivity gains

Economists are too often obsessed with equilibrium: the balance of supply and demand. They imagine perfectly competitive markets based on perfect information. Technology comes from the outside and leaves the basic proportions of their models unchanged. Productivity growth, however, is never smooth; it is always the result of dynamic and disruptive processes.

To get a better sense of what is involved it is more useful to look at the heterodox economic tradition. Part of this tradition comes from the Left and from Marx. For Marx, capital is always on the move, in search of what he called its "self-expansion". Companies are compelled to invest, and by investing to expand and survive. "Accumulate, accumulate! That is Moses and the Prophets!" This has nothing to do with the psychology of the capitalists. The drive is systemic. And as companies and capitals accumulate, so they have to innovate. Marx, of course, saw any success as self-limiting, and exploitative. But in his focus on the dynamics of movement in capitalism he was far ahead of the other economists of his day.

Significant elements of Marx's thinking were and are shared by the so-called Austrian economists, although they turned the arguments politically in a more conservative direction. Joseph Schumpeter was the giant here. "Capitalism", he wrote, "is by nature a form or method of economic change and not only never is but never can be stationary" (Schumpeter 1976

[1943]: 82). Writing decades after Marx's death, he was more immersed in the academic world but he nevertheless rejected the dominant strain of economic thinking that focused on equilibrium and perfect competition. He has had a powerful impact on our understanding of central aspects of productivity change.

To see the differences between the conventional and the more heterodox approaches we can look at their reflection (albeit a pale one) in the distinction between two types of productivity gains: static productivity gains and dynamic productivity gains.

Figure 2.2 shows a production possibility frontier (PPF). This is an imaginary line that represents the maximum we could get if we employed all our resources as efficiently as possible with a given technology and knowledge. It is a line of "ideal efficiency" at a specific point in time. Without more assumptions we cannot know where we would be on the line PPFt, but the line itself can be theorized in terms of the perfect competition model. Assume, for the sake of argument, that point A represents perfect efficiency at time $t$. Of course, we know that no economy is ever perfectly efficient.

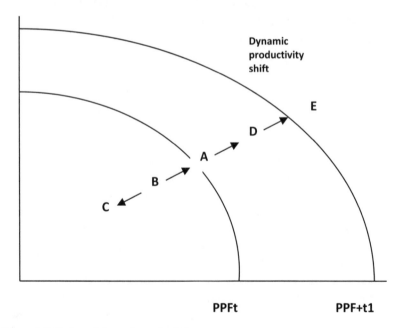

**Figure 2.2** Static and dynamic productivity

There will be a *resource utilization problem*: for structural and cyclical reasons capital and labour may be unemployed or underemployed. There is a *resource allocation problem*: we may employ resources in the wrong areas. And there is a resource *intensity of use problem*: "firms" may not be squeezing the most out of the resources they use. Instead of being at A our real economy may be at B. If we move the economy from B closer to the ideal point A then this will improve productivity. Since we can only do this once, this is called a *static productivity gain*.

Economists have spent a huge amount of time theorizing and extending the perfect competition model to explain the imaginary world on the frontier PPFt. They can then change the assumptions to see how we are pulled to less efficient states below the curve. This kind of thinking encourages them to believe that more flexible markets will make a big difference. But over half a century ago this idea was exploded by what is called "the theory of the second best" (Lipsey & Lancaster 1956). It was shown that while some market imperfections may add to one another and force you further below the curve, others can sometimes cancel one another out, perhaps even moving you closer to the curve. If you removed all the imperfections then you would move to a state of perfect efficiency, but if you only remove some you may end up in a worse position. You could go not from B to A but B to C. Unfortunately, there is no *a priori* way in which you can know which is the more likely.

How big is any static inefficiency gap in the real world? This is a problem too. In the 1950s the economist Arnold Harberger, a free market enthusiast, showed that the deadweight "welfare" loss created by market distortions could be represented diagrammatically as a "triangle" on the familiar supply and demand diagram. This can be seen in Figure 2.3a. Because of market distortions the amount supplied falls from Qe to Qdw and prices rise from Pe to Pdw. This opens up the deadweight triangle. But when he estimated these welfare losses empirically his numbers seemed small. This was especially so compared to lost output when the economy moved away from its full employment potential. This is illustrated in Figure 2.3b, where the ideal full employment path of the economy is compared to its real path.

This gap is sometimes called the "Okun gap" after another economist – Arthur Okun. Both "failings" will produce output losses and therefore productivity losses. But which is the bigger? It seems likely that the output and productivity losses from capitalism's ups and downs will far outweigh

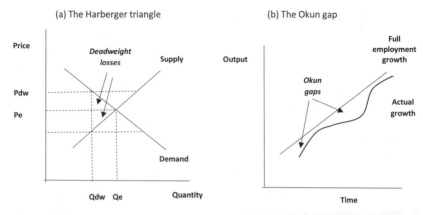

**Figure 2.3** Two types of economic losses

those Harberger identified. Or, as James Tobin once put it, "it takes a heap of Harberger Triangles to fill an Okun Gap" (Tobin 1977: 468).

The real vigour of capitalism comes more from dynamic productivity gains. These involve applying better knowledge to changing "technologies" in their widest sense. The result is that the production possibility frontier moves outwards over time, in our diagram from PPFt to PPF+t1, possibly from A to E. But as we know that we will never be on either of these frontiers, the real movement is more likely to be from B to D. This is what happens every day in capitalism. It is hard empirically to separate out static and dynamic gain, the balance of which in any case is likely to vary in time and place. But there is something more important. What if a degree of static inefficiency is necessary to achieve a higher degree of dynamic efficiency?

One way in which this might happen is in terms of the short-termism of the static model. This is especially important for economic development (Blaug 2001). A useful way of thinking about this is in terms of the pursuit curve shown in Figure 2.4. Imagine you are cycling along a path through a field and suddenly a ferocious dog begins to chase you. As the dog starts to run you peddle faster. The dog tries to get to where you are as quickly as possible but each time it looks up you have moved on. So, its pursuit path – which looks rational in the short run – turns out to be less rational in the long run.

You can easily guess that the cyclist represents the moving economic competitors and the dog is the company, region or economy trying to catch

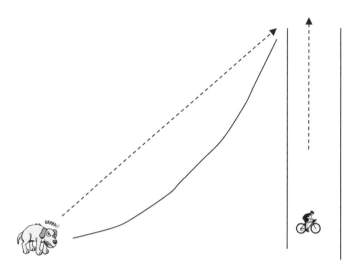

**Figure 2.4** The pursuit curve

them up. The focus on immediate gains at the expense of those that are longer term is one of the ways in which "market" theorizing defeats itself as a recipe for change and development. But the issue is not simply one of what is more technically called your "time horizon", it also involves questions about structural change.

## Sector shifts

An important part of the story of productivity change involves the process of structural change. Structural change is the movement of resources from agriculture to industry and on to services. Take a simple example. Suppose that labour productivity is 100 per cent higher in industry than in agriculture. If this is reflected in the wage rate, and if workers in the countryside are free to move, then structural change will occur. The overall productivity rate will rise because a greater share of the labour force is now in a higher-productivity sector. This means that we can expect economies that are developing to have faster rates of growth than those which are already developed because the most advanced economies will already have exhausted many of the opportunities for structural change. Growth paths, and the record of productivity changes within them, will look like an aeroplane taking off but then eventually levelling off. The resulting curve will have an S shape. Such S-shaped curves are very important in real life. They reflect the fact that things cannot go on increasing at the same rate forever.

Some economists treat these structural changes as examples of static gains. But structural change is one of the most dynamic elements in productivity change and economic growth. It is driven not by static differences so much as dynamic changes in comparative productivity growth rates between sectors. Just think of some of the processes involved. When labour is pushed or pulled out of agriculture it involves massive social changes. Eric Hobsbawm once said these had three elements: land must become a commodity; it must pass into the hands of a class willing to use it for profit; and "peasants" must become "free wage labourers" (Hobsbawm 1962). This, often bitter, transformation is still going on in some parts of the world. Structural change involves mass migration, urbanization, bustling cities, bright lights and huge social and infrastructural problems that need to be dealt with. It is a central part of the economic history of successful developing countries and the story of their productivity growth.

Economists often dislike the messiness of such big stories. If they can reduce things to the bare essentials then they like to do so. The best-known attempt to "theorize" the central element of this process of structural change is associated with Nicholas Kaldor. Economists and economic historians had long seen "manufacturing" as an engine of growth, but Kaldor formalized the arguments into seven "laws" or perhaps propositions. Two are especially important. The first is the insight (taken from the work of Allyn Young and Petrus Verdoorn) that manufacturing productivity growth will be higher because of increasing returns to scale. The second is that this will then induce more speedy shifts of labour from agriculture to industry so that "the faster the rate of growth of manufacturing output, the faster the rate of growth of productivity in the economy *as a whole*" (Thirlwall 1983). This means that we would expect to see an increase in the rate of productivity growth as a country developed and then a decrease as it matured (Kaldor's immediate concern was Britain in the 1960s). Kaldor's laws were quickly seen to be important in explaining the differences in growth and productivity rates between the advanced countries after the Second World War, then the patterns of rapid change in some poorer countries – first the

USSR and Japan, and then the Asian Tigers and on to China today. We shall return to these ideas in Chapters 5–7.

Is it possible for productivity change to work the other way? Might the overall rate of productivity growth be reduced by labour moving from a more productive sector to a less productive one? The answer is yes. This too is an important part of the story of productivity growth. It has worked in different ways depending on whether we are looking at the advanced or less advanced world. In the advanced world, industry's share in output and the labour force rose to very high levels but has now fallen and been overtaken by the service sector. Today in the advanced economies the proportion of labour in services is around 80 per cent. Services tend to be labour-intensive. While Kaldor was evoking his "laws" about manufacturing growth and productivity, William Baumol was developing related ideas about structural change and services. You cannot, he said, improve the productivity of an orchestra or a string quarter by reducing the number of players. Why would you want to if you like live music? This simple insight led him to think about how, in advanced economies, we might choose to devote more and more resources to things like face-to-face health care, social care and education, where the possibility of labour-saving productivity gains is limited. This would lower productivity growth. If we value some things more than others this would be no bad thing (Baumol & Bowen 1966; Baumol 2012). Does this include everything in the service sector? Not all labour there seems equally useful. Where it is not, we could eliminate the tasks or improve productivity by "mechanizing" them or computerizing them. Any reader in the caring professions can read on with better heart. Artificial intelligence may be beginning to have a role in medical diagnosis but who wants a computerized robot carer? On the other hand, if you happen to be one of the 1.3 million accountants in the US or the 300,000 or so in the UK, you might find the job threat of a computerized accountant raising productivity a little more threatening.

Such dilemmas are hardly likely to impress people in developing countries looking for productivity growth to drive their economies forwards. There the problem has been the dramatic growth of the urban informal sector where people survive through forms of petty trade and production. From the 1980s there was a move to open up developing economies that reflected the ideas of the "Washington Consensus", the policy effectively triangulated by the World Bank, the International Monetary Fund (IMF) and the US Treasury. Competition from inside and outside would force businesses to improve to survive. But it drove many out of business and stalled the growth of labour in the manufacturing sectors. Workers who lost their jobs either became unemployed or more likely semi-employed in the informal sector. This also became the destination of many rural–urban migrants. For Latin America, one account suggests that productivity gains within sectors rose at just under 2 per cent on average for nearly 50 years. But from the 1950s to 1975 productivity was given an additional boost by positive structural change which contributed another 2 per cent of growth per year. Between 1990 and 2005, however, structural change flipped, and at −0.2 per cent per year it reduced the overall rate of productivity growth. This reversal has been called "astounding". It is not the only example (McMillan *et al.* 2014). In Chapter 7 we shall look at the experience of Africa, where we see some evidence of a reversal on no less a scale.

## Invention, innovation and diffusion

It is common to break down the processes of "technological change" into three elements. *Invention* is about the creation of new products and processes. *Innovation* is the commercial application of these. *Diffusion* is the take-up of innovations across an area: for example, an industry or national economy. Each of them has their own characteristics, even what have been called "environmental contingencies". Being able to think "outside of the box" to create new things is not easy. Nor is turning good ideas into commercial applications. James Dyson is famous, for example, for massively improving the vacuum cleaner. But it is said to have taken over 5,000 prototypes to get something that could be sold. Only the most advanced economies will have the resources and networks to support this. Technological change is, therefore, likely to flow from the more advanced to the less advanced economies.

We can think about diffusion in terms of another S-shaped curve. Figure 2.5 sets out an example: the S-shaped curve here shows the cumulative take-up of a new product or process; slow at the start, then faster and then slower as it is taken up by the laggards. On the right we see the diffusion process mapped in take-up levels over time. The shape of these curves varies between products, processes and, crucially, economies. This means that at any point in time there will be a variety of products and processes in

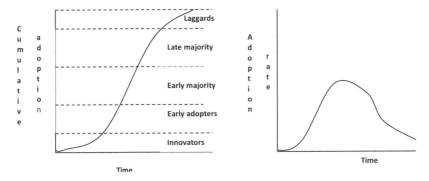

**Figure 2.5** Innovation diffusion curves for new products and processes

use so that any productivity figure, for more than the smallest unit, will be an average of these different elements. And since the capitalist economy is dynamic, both best practices and the composition of the average behind it will be changing over time. The explanation of the extent and unevenness of diffusion (and even possible regressions) is also one where conventional economics focusing on abstract market models – perfect and imperfect – will again not be helpful.

## Creative destruction

One of the most famous phrases used to describe the process by which capitalism becomes more productive is that of *creative destruction*. It is the central idea of Joseph Schumpeter. He seems to have got the term from Werner Sombart who in turn borrowed it from Friedrich Nietzsche. Capitalism produces "the perennial gale of creative destruction". "Creative Destruction is the essential fact about capitalism. It is what capitalism consists in and what every capitalist concern has got to live in" (Schumpeter 1976 [1943]: 83–4).

Productivity shifts are often associated with huge breakthroughs: trains, boats and planes. These are examples of big creative destruction. It is now fashionable to talk of "general purpose technologies", think steam power, electricity, maybe computing (Bresnahan & Trajtenberg 1995). Such technologies bring large quantitative and qualitative improvements in themselves, but have wider consequences too; consider the change from candles to oil lamps and then to electric lighting. General purpose technologies are defined by the breadth of their impact, by their capacity for continued improvement and by the way they lead to "innovational complementarities" (spillovers) into the creation of new processes, products and services. In some ways this is a return to an older view of the nature and impact of technological change. In the 1960s it became fashionable to debunk the impact of a general purpose technology like the railway by estimating "social rates of return" and imagining how developments might have occurred had such a technology not developed. These studies, dubious perhaps in principle, also tended to focus on measuring change in a certain year, whereas today the emphasis on general purpose technologies stresses their cumulative and broadening effect over time. Take the steam engine in Britain as an example. There had been steam engines before Boulton and Watt's first commercially produced ones which date from 1776. Near a hundred years later, in 1870, there seemed to be an impressive million steam engine horse power in use. But steam engines were still mainly confined to railways, mining and the textile industry. Move forwards to 1907 and there was an astonishing 10 million steam engine horse power in use. Steam had become generalized, but the bigger generalization only came in the second century after the original commercial breakthrough (Musson 1976; Kanefsky 1979).

This is of more than historical interest. The argument is that it takes a long time for the full productivity-enhancing effects of big technological shifts to work through. The same delays can be seen in the impact of the development of electricity, and of transport development linked to motor vehicles. They can be seen too in the delays in the impact of the development of the aeroplane, and so on. Those who take this view then argue that we need to beware underestimating the impact of the productivity-enhancing change linked to computers, information technology and digitalization. Developments here go back a half century or more, but it might still be too soon to judge the scale of their transformative impact, much of which may not yet be felt. We might be making the same mistake as people did if they judged steam power by its spread in 1870 rather than 1914.

Big gains can also come from more mundane changes: small creative destruction. Economists argue that the more open trade is, the more productive will be the use of the world's resources. An important element in enabling the growth of global trade in the last half century has been something as seemingly simple as the container: a big metal box. Productivity too is about the world inside the home. The availability of things like washing machines, fridges and microwaves means that less time needs to be spent on household tasks, so releasing labour for other things or for leisure. Ha-Joon Chang has suggested that by releasing women from the home (yes, a lot of productivity writing has pretty conventional views) the washing machine has made a bigger productivity contribution than the internet (Chang 2011: 31–40). Things also improve by even smaller changes over time: the story of the computer chip is now the classic example.

It would be interesting to know where the real centre of gravity of productivity change lies: does it come from big changes or the accumulation of many smaller ones? It is hard to measure these things directly. However, it seems probable that *in the shorter term* the bigger role is played by existing firms improving what they do rather than disruptions of new technologies offered by new firms. One study, using employment data, has suggested that in the past half century around 25 per cent of growth can be attributed to new firms doing new things and 75 per cent to improvements within established companies and new varieties of existing products. No less interesting, the role of big creative destruction by doing new things declined in these data from 27 per cent in 1976–86 to 19 per cent between 2003 and 2013 (Garcia-Macia *et al.* 2016).

There is another issue about productivity growth and technical change that needs to be raised here. If capitalism drives technological change forwards, are some kinds of change preferred to others? This is an argument about the ways in which capitalism may also constrain the choices made. Businesses, for example, want changes that enhance profits. Pharmaceutical companies have been accused of prioritizing marketing over research and development, and spending more on developing drugs for pampered rich world pets than medicines for the ills of the world's poor. Consumers with empty pockets are less attractive than those with full ones. It has long been argued, too, that businesses will prefer techniques that reinforce their control of, and reduce their dependence on, labour, rather than strengthen the position of labour. Indeed, some argue that "labour control" has been a major factor in both wider organizational and narrower technical choices. They prefer technologies that strengthen their position against their competitors and mitigate against cooperative technologies. They then try to maximize their competitive positions by controlling such technologies through commercial secrecy and the use and proliferation of patents and other forms of control of information. Such arguments not only raise questions about past patterns, but also the appropriateness of institutions today and their ability to take us forwards tomorrow.

## The role of the entrepreneur in productivity growth

The observant reader will have noticed that we have not said much about real people so far. If economists tend to treat technological change as "manna from heaven", they have no explanation of agency: who does what? "*The theoretical firm is entrepreneur-less*", said William Baumol, who spent much of his life trying to stretch the conventional economic framework to include the idea of entrepreneurship (Baumol 1968: 66).

It was again Joseph Schumpeter who gave force to the argument that entrepreneurship is a key factor in productivity change. A tedious debate has since flowed as to how to define an entrepreneur, which we will not explore here. Suffice it to say that for Schumpeter an entrepreneur was neither an inventor nor an innovator but a mobilizer: someone who got things done.

> The function of entrepreneurs is to reform or revolutionize the pattern of production by exploiting an invention, or more generally an untried technological possibility for producing a new commodity or producing an old one in a new way, by opening up a new source of supply of materials or a new outlet for products, by reorganizing an industry and so on. (Schumpeter 1976 [1943]: 132)

The paradox is that Schumpeter thought that this model of the dynamic mobilizer was becoming less relevant. In modern capitalism the individual entrepreneurial function was being marginalized by the rise of big business. Schumpeter saw big companies as inevitable. He recognized that creative destruction might eventually force some of them under but he still lauded their contribution to progress. New firms come into existence too and grow, sometimes spectacularly as with recent new technology companies like Apple and Google. However, technical and organizational change was more likely to come from the competition of existing firms doing old things better and moving into doing new things. This is how some of the most dynamic survive. Nokia, for example, was founded in 1865 and has moved from running a pulp mill in the paper industry to producing rubber and cables, then on to phones and telecommunications infrastructure. Others have shifted away from producing things to providing services. General Electric traces its roots back to Thomas Edison but is now a huge conglomerate whose reach extends over a huge range of products and services. "Technological progress has become the business of teams of trained scientists who turn out what is required and make it work in predictable ways". "Innovation is being reduced to a routine" (Schumpeter 1976 [1943]: 132).

One measure of this is the distribution of research and development spending as an input to productivity growth. This tends to be highly skewed to richer countries: they can afford it. Within them it is then skewed to bigger firms. The US data in Table 2.3 are helpful here and confirm what may be intuitively obvious. It puts the argument for the role of individual small-scale entrepreneurs into perspective.

It is important then to distinguish the reality of entrepreneurship from what Scott Shane has called its "folklore". Shane points to a mass of evidence which suggests that the higher the level of economic development, the less individual entrepreneurs are likely to succeed. The real productivity dynamism of the US economy does not seem to derive from its "entrepreneurial

**Table 2.3** US company distribution of R&D by number of employees, 2008–15 (%)

| No. employees | 2008 | 2015 |
|---|---|---|
| *Large scale* | | |
| +25,000 | 34.7 | 35.6 |
| 10,000–24,999 | 16.7 | 16.8 |
| 5,000–9,999 | 8.5 | 10.9 |
| 1,000–4,999 | 15.9 | 16.3 |
| 250–999 | 7.6 | 8.1 |
| *Medium* | | |
| 50–249 | 8.2 | 7.0 |
| *Small* | | |
| < 49 | 8.3 | 5.3 |

*Source*: https://nsf.gov/statistics/2018/nsb20181/report/sections/research-and-development-u-s-trends-and-international-comparisons/u-s-business-r-d.

culture". "America is no longer a particularly entrepreneurial country", the number of US entrepreneurial start-ups "has been flat or declining over the past twenty years". (This turns out to be true of all rich economies.) In fact, the US has the third lowest start-up rate in the OECD. The openings created by big shifts may be shorter lived. Silicon Valley is below average for start-ups. The typical start-up in the US "is a low-tech endeavour, like a construction company or an auto repair shop" or "a personal service, a hair salon or a clothing store". "Every year only about 7 percent of new companies in the United States are started in ... high technology, and only about 3 percent of business founders consider their new businesses to be 'technologically sophisticated.'" These conclusions are easily replicated across the advanced world (Shane 2008).

Can the argument about small-scale entrepreneurship be saved? William Baumol thought so. He recognized, as most commentators do, that technological change arises from three sources in modern capitalism: the work of small-scale inventors and innovators as entrepreneurs, that of big companies and the supporting assistance of the state (and, within it, modern universities). To get around the argument that big oligopolistic businesses have taken over innovation, he argued that there is "David and Goliath" symbiosis in which the original big breakthroughs come from the "Davids" but it is the "Goliaths", the big corporations, that routinize continuous improvement once the breakthrough had occurred (Baumol 2002). Baumol's evidence base for this seems weak and unsystematic and, as we will see later, this idea conflicts with arguments about other aspects of "productivity puzzles". Rather than trying to save the role of the small entrepreneur, it makes more sense to look not only at what big business does but also the role of the state in all its forms.

Conventional economic wisdom suggests that the state should, in the words of *The Economist* magazine, "stick to the basics". In terms of productivity and technological change, this means providing a positive climate for private initiative, a good infrastructure and then "leav[ing] the rest to the [private sector] revolutionaries". A minority tradition argues that in reality state support for innovation and productivity growth is everywhere. Ignoring it theoretically means misunderstanding the limits of the role of the private sector, ignoring it in practice means misunderstanding what actually happens in capitalism. This argument has been more fully set out by Mariana Mazzucato in *The Entrepreneurial State* (2013). She argues that the state plays an extensive role in technological change, and the bigger the changes, the bigger its role. The positive role of the state has been especially important in the way it has supported the development of new general purpose technologies, including the internet and digital technologies. In the US, no less than Europe, there is a huge gap between the rhetoric of the market and the reality of the role of "the advanced development state":

> we continue to romanticize private actors in innovative industries, ignoring their dependence on the products of public investment. Elon Musk, for example, has not only received over $5 billion in subsidies from the US government; his companies, SpaceX and Tesla, have been built on the work of NASA and the Department of Energy, respectively. (Mazzucato 2018b)

Where the market is more limited there will be less private investment in research and development. There will also be a problem the bigger, deeper and more extreme the uncertainty. If risk and possible rewards cannot be easily estimated, businesses will prefer investment for more incremental changes that produce shorter-term profits rather than more speculative investment that might (or might not) lead to really fundamental changes. The result, Mazzucato suggests, is that "the private sector is in many ways less entrepreneurial than the public sector: it shies away from radically new products and processes, leaving the most uncertain investments to be first taken on by the State" (Mazzucato 2013: 67).

States invest in basic research; they support many development costs; they subsidize companies directly, and offer tax advantages and grants; they support demand through government procurement and through the support of private demand; and they play a much more central role in infrastructure development than is often acknowledged. States invest too in the development of transport systems, housing developments, etc., which are then a condition for productivity gains elsewhere.

The failure to recognize this positive role of the state, Mazzucato argues, has also contributed towards recent stagnationist tendencies in productivity growth. Without a positive state vision, the capacity to "think big" is despised; it is seen to be legitimate to privatize the gains of positive state action while socializing the risks ("public investment ... becomes business giveaways", Mazzucato 2013: 19); the state's capacity to tax is undermined by reduced taxes on businesses and easier tax evasion, and its capacity to lead change is undermined by bureaucratic weakening; and within the private sector companies are allowed to prioritize short-run profits gained by financial manipulation over longer-run investment for big productivity-enhancing research and development.

## Creative destruction versus destructive destruction

A question that is too rarely posed is how big is the *creation* in any creative destruction compared to the *destruction* (Komlos 2016)? We have seen that the most important changes are the most disruptive. They deliver major new products or services, make old products dramatically better and cheaper and in so doing make a significant and clear contribution to real productivity growth. But is this true, for example, of all new products? Some years ago, economists noticed that there seemed to be an increasing variety of products appearing. Measuring new products is not easy, but one study suggested that variety was increasing at around 1 per cent per year with the rate having sped up. Perhaps, economists reasoned, productivity growth was understated because of the failure to take this increasing variety into account. Some got even more excited when another study by John Hausman claimed to demonstrate a much larger economic benefit to consumers from the introduction of apple and cinnamon flavoured Cheerios (I am serious) than had previously been thought possible (Hausman 1997). Sceptics thought that if you have a theory and a model that leads you to think that a new unhealthy breakfast cereal is significantly adding to hidden welfare gains then perhaps you need a different theory and model. When Hausman first wrote, the number of breakfast cereals in the US seemed to have doubled in the previous two decades to over 300. In the next two decades they seemingly increased tenfold to over 4,000 and today include 17 varieties of Cheerios alone. A more realistic view would seem to be that such new product development is based on spurious and even regressive forms of differentiation. Inferior goods are sold as superior, identical goods differentiated. When this happens "new products" can be disruptive without adding anything to any sensible measure of human welfare.

Even when differences are more genuine, technologies that are close substitutes can be disruptive without necessarily delivering much gain. In my lifetime I have bought expensive record players and built a vinyl collection. I have junked them in favour of cassette tapes and players. These made way for a CD collection which in turn made way for digital files and specialized MP3 players. Then came files on phones and music streaming. Each of these changes involved such close substitutes that the gains seem limited (and, if we are to believe the enthusiasts for vinyl, nothing has yet outdone its quality of reproduction). The gain is also less if the "newness" involves a degree of planned obsolescence.

Despite his argument that capitalism is a "free-market innovation machine", Baumol also drew our attention to its dark side. Entrepreneurship, he argued, might be productive but it could also be unproductive and some of it destructive. He thought that there was nothing constructive about the effort and entrepreneurship applied to making criminal gains. But even within the law some entrepreneurs depend on activities that involve a "parasitical existence that is actually damaging to the economy" (Baumol 1990: 894). Businesses might try to exploit forms of rent seeking and to grab the benefits of real productivity growth that others are generating. This is exactly what some argue has been happening in the financial sector in recent decades. Famously, in 2009 Aidar Turner, then head of the British Financial Services Authority, complained that "the City" had become too big. It was disruptive but it was also, he said, "socially useless". He initially made this argument about what he called "the exotica" of banking with its alphabet soup of doubtful "securities". He has since developed it into a critique of the way that everyday lending practices can undermine stability too (Turner 2016).

When creative destruction occurs, capital and stocks of things also become redundant. Some capital may be transferred but much of it is embodied in ways that mean it is too specific to recycle or be turned into something else. Labour too is affected by the destructive side. There may be net technological unemployment. Even if this does not occur, workers may be forced to shift down to deskilled work at lower wages. This can affect cities, regions and whole economies. Schumpeter was aware of this problem. He talked of the need for winners to compensate losers either directly *or*, more logically, through the state. Unfortunately, as Stephen Marglin puts it, "compensation is not forthcoming and how do you compensate somebody for the destruction of the community in which she grew up, is raising a family, and hopes one day to retire and look after her grandchildren … ?" (Marglin 2010: 10).

By now we have hopefully established the dynamics of productivity change and the limits of our understanding. Before we dig any deeper, we need to turn in Chapter 3 to the fraught question of how to measure productivity improvement.

# 3

# Mysterious figures

Productivity appears to be a simple calculation, but what do we measure and how do we add things together? This chapter is about these numbers and how they are arrived at. Sounds boring? Let us try again. This is a chapter about whether we should measure cooking, toilet training, sex, drugs and "rock and roll", and how. It is about discrimination and misogyny. It is about tax dodging, cheating and lying, even cooking the "national books". It is also about the new layers of complexity that are growing as a result of the organizational shift from creating new value to forms of "rent seeking". Debt seems to be everywhere. State licences create "illusory" value in intellectual property. Modern business is rife with subsidy extraction. Tax dodging is endemic, speculation commonplace (Standing 2016; Mazzucato 2018a). Capitalism is moving ever further away from any textbook model and everyone is struggling more to get the "data" and to make sense of it to logically and to consistently measure real outputs and real inputs. Things are not as simple as they might seem.

## Measuring matters

For thousands of years, day-to-day measurements were done by rule of thumb, sometimes using local measures. Even everyday conceptions of time were vague. The rise of capitalism demanded more precision. This was partly a question of technology, but it was also an economic requirement. Companies wanted to know their accounts and new states their populations. Common national and international systems of physical measurement were developed. Pioneers began to ask questions about what the size of outputs and inputs might be in a "nation": not just the population but the size of the labour force, the area of land being farmed and the total amount of coal or iron being produced. Investigators became interested in understanding the ways in which tools were being used and machine production organized. Charles Babbage, having thought about the basic idea of a computer, perhaps in anticipation of the idea of garbage in–garbage out, was anxious to accurately describe, measure and count what went on in workshops and factories in early nineteenth-century Britain.

The pioneers were interested in the intellectual challenge of doing the economic measuring and trying to understand the economy as a process of inputs and outputs. It was only in the twentieth century that these led to an interest in productivity calculations, and especially those related to the national economy or parts of it. This new concern was partly a product of the development of Keynesian economic theory and its focus on the macroeconomy. It was driven much more by the need to plan the war effort between 1939 and 1945 and then arguments about economic growth. These led to the development of clearer concepts of outputs and inputs and to the creation of state statistical agencies which would collect the data. In the UK, for example, statistical units originally grew up attached to different government ministries and local government units. It was only the needs of war in 1941 that forced the creation of the Central Statistical Office to help plan the war effort and to resolve what Churchill called "the utmost confusion ... caused when people argue on different statistical data". Only in 1996 were all the statistical functions of the government brought together in the Office for National Statistics, which then had some 3,000 employees and today has nearer 4,500 (Pullinger 1997).

But how are things actually measured? Economic statistics have been said to be like sausage: it is better not to ask how it is made. The classic study of the "accuracy", or rather inaccuracy, of economic observation was made decades ago by Oscar Morgenstern (Morgenstern 1963). As a postgraduate I was warned not to read it because I would never do anything again. I rejected the advice, but ever since I have had great respect for those who try to measure and who are also not afraid to discuss the limitations of what they do.

Take a simple physical productivity measure like the average crop yield per hectare in the UK. To calculate this, we need to know the total area planted and the weight of the harvest. We might be able to measure this for a farm, but no one could measure all the land used and weigh all the harvest nationally. Instead surveys are used. Assume everyone tells the truth, what truth do we want them to tell? Do we estimate the weight of the harvest in the field or measure it in the barn? If the latter, how do we deal with the complications of "impurities" and moisture content, etc.? Then how do we measure the total land input? In a poor country it is even more difficult. Maybe in the case of this yield example satellite data about land use and estimated harvest size in the field will be more accurate than survey data produced on the ground. If measuring tangible inputs and outputs like land and grain turns out to be harder than it might appear, this is even more the case when it comes to measuring intangible inputs and outputs like knowledge and ideas, including the value of "rock and roll".

The most secure basis for measurement is census data, although the most cursory history of any census will quickly disabuse any reader of overconfidence in its results. Population censuses are the most regularly carried out, but there have also been censuses of production and distribution. Unfortunately, censuses are always years and sometimes decades apart. In the most advanced countries the basic data are therefore collected by national statistical organizations on a monthly, quarterly and annual basis. They draw on data produced by the state as part of its day-to-day functions, for example taxation and expenditure, and they draw on regular surveys of output, prices and labour. Such surveys are only ever as good as their sample size and the rigour with which all aspects are carried out. It is also common to draw on estimates for missing data and sometimes plain guesstimates.

No aggregate data will ever be better than its component parts. No serious scientist or engineer proceeds as if measurement errors cancel each other out. As a rule we can say that the more developed the economy, the better the data. Yet the possibility of significant measurement error is still real and is too often ignored until something thought to be suspicious emerges. The less developed the economy, whether now or in the past, the more the balance tips towards the less reliable type of measurement, a narrower range of lower-quality data and, in the worst cases, guessing. Today the minimum data required to estimate national output and its main components for poor countries is said to be surveys of enterprise performance, trade and sales, household surveys and price surveys. In the most advanced economies much more data are used. Eurostat, the statistical agency of the European Union, lists some 20 different surveys, all with huge but varying coverage, most monthly, that go into their output and input calculations.

In these surveys an additional issue will be price. Price, remember, is our common denominator whether trying to add up inputs or outputs. Getting at everyday price data is not always easy. More attention has always been paid to consumer or retail prices. But covering the variation that exists can be difficult. There is often said to be a big capital city effect, especially in poor countries, because that is where the data are most easily collected. The prices of inputs are even more difficult to collect. Wages are less of a problem than the price of capital goods, whatever the economy we are looking at. There is still some truth in Zvi Griliches' old observation that the price statistics of capital goods are "orphans in the world of social statistics" (quoted in Gould 1972: 297). This makes any attempt to calculate the capital input and capital productivity a problem.

Once we have the price data we then have to deal with the problem of inflation and changing relative prices over time within an economy. Price data are collected in the prices of the day: current prices. To measure productivity changes, we need to use constant prices. This is usually done by deflating or removing the effects of inflation (and occasionally deflation). We get the deflated price index by measuring how the price of a range of goods changes over time. But because of the breadth of what goes into GDP, the way this is done must be broader than that used to measure consumer inflation. Relative prices will also be changing. When an economy is changing fast, it makes a big difference whether we use what are called early or late year relative prices. Suppose we choose an early year. Then there will be no prices for things that have not yet been developed and high prices for new things that are relatively scarce. If we choose a late (more recent) year we will have poor prices for things no longer in demand and the once newer things, if they are now common, will be relatively cheaper. The case of the USSR became notorious. When GDP growth between 1928 and 1937 was measured in 1928 prices it was found to be 271 per cent. But measured in 1937 prices it was 162 per cent (Davies 1998: 39). When comparing rates of change we will always get different results depending on which base we choose. There are ways of trying to get around this problem but over the longer period statisticians do have to change or "rebase" how they do their calculations. Intermittent rebasing creates especially serious problems with the data when economies experience faster growth (think China) or when there are long gaps between the changes (think Africa).

The value data we get from these measurements will still be in national currencies – pounds, dollars, euros, Chinese renminbi, Japanese yen. How do we make international comparisons? We could use the currency exchange rate to create dollar comparisons. (Once it would have been comparisons in sterling reflecting the power of British capitalism – now it is dollars because of American dominance.) However, the exchange rate is determined by the international trade in goods and services of an economy and, if an exchange rates floats, it will be constantly moving. The prices of goods traded internationally will tend to be closer to one another. This is not true of domestically traded goods. These are less affected by international competition. Haircuts is the example often given. When we travel, we quickly realize that the exchange rate we get is only a partial guide to whether things are cheaper or dearer for us in the countries we visit. A Turkish barber in London or New York, for example, is a lot more expensive than one in Turkey. To solve this problem we can calculate values using what are called purchasing power parities (PPPs). PPPs (they are usually abbreviated) are artificial exchange rates in "international dollars" that try to take account of the domestic price differences. The more advanced the economy, the closer the PPP figures of output will be to those calculated using exchange rates. The less advanced the economy, the greater the gap. You can check this out by looking at China and seeing the difference between its output calculated using market exchange rates and its PPP figures. It is not that one is right and the other wrong. The two figures are measuring different things. It is, however, important to remember that you cannot buy anything internationally with PPP values. What counts when you buy and sell abroad is exchange rates.

Measuring is only part of the problem. We then need to work through the logic of what to include and what not to include and how to add up our data and correct for any missing elements.

## The rise of the GDP rule book

Today when we think of total output we usually think of GDP. GDP is the standard measure of output for a national economy which is used to calculate overall productivity change. Because of the richness of the data that go into its calculation, its subcomponents can provide much of the data of outputs and inputs for narrower productivity calculations: the productivity of sectors, industries, regions, even cities. Over time the number of countries for which GDP data have become available has grown, but many countries still do not have much beyond the basics and the series are often short. Even so, the concept of GDP has been said by the US Department of Commerce to be one of the "greatest inventions of the twentieth century" (Lepenies 2016: x).

GDP measures what is produced domestically as opposed to gross national product, which also includes the net earnings from abroad (profits, dividends, interest, wages). There are three ways of measuring total output. The *production approach* adds up the value of everything that is produced minus the inputs needed to produce it, effectively a value-added approach. The *income approach* adds up everything that is earned: wages, profits, rents and interest. The *expenditure approach* adds together the market value of spending on final goods by consumers, businesses and the government together with exports minus imports. Since these all focus in different aspects of the same economic mechanism – production, incomes, consumption – they should give the same result. They do not because each has its own measurement problems. In most cases the production approach is the dominant one because it is simply easier to do (Landefeld *et al.* 2008).

To make sense of the problems of productivity calculations and the GDP numerator we need to continually keep in mind the big complications set out in Chapter 1. But even if we accept the narrower logic of national income accounting, we soon find it is a bit like the "rabbit hole" in *Alice in Wonderland*. Go down it and we encounter a bewildering world that at times can look crazy even in its own terms. There are logical problems about what to include and how. There are problems over whether prices adequately capture what we want to know. We will also find problems about whether outputs (and inputs) are being correctly allocated to the right parts of the system. Having reviewed some of these problems, Diane Coyle still argues that "GDP, for all its faults, is still a bright light shining through the mist" (Coyle 2015: 145). Jacob Assa, on the other hand, wonders if national accounts "can be considered statistics at all" (Assa 2017). The question of whether we can trust "the numbers" is coming back with a vengeance.

We owe our basic ideas about how to calculate output to a group of pioneering economists, including Colin Clark and Simon Kuznets, working in the 1920s and 1930s. They struggled with the basic ideas but also a series of conundrums that adding up output presented. "Strict logic is a stern master, and if one respected it, one would never construct or use any production index", said Arthur Burns, another of the pioneers of trying to measure national production (quoted in Schumpeter 1976 [1943]: 63). When it came to producing a codified system of calculations during the Second World War and immediately after the war, many earlier concerns were marginalized. Later Richard Stone was awarded the Nobel Prize for his pioneering work in leading this new codification. The codification often seemed to involve arbitrary solutions, and doubts about this have never gone away. The British and US states valued the calculations being done in specific ways. "Power drives measurement", says Assa in his account (Assa 2017). It certainly wins arguments.

The first general manual for the system of national accounts was issued in 1953. Updates followed in 1968, 1993 and 2008. These updates were a product of the growing cooperation of statisticians from the United Nations, OECD, European Union, IMF and World Bank. Each update became longer and more complex – expanding from 45 pages to over 700 in the latest. In theory all countries should follow the rules in these manuals. Some do not and make this explicit. Such comparative inconsistencies would matter less if one of these countries was not the US. It would also matter less if so much productivity analysis did not make large claims on the basis of small differences in the data. Other countries who do follow the manuals may not all do so with the same care. This is especially the case if they lack resources, as most poor countries do.

The current advice on how to calculate output is set out in the 2008 system of national accounts. The key passage is this one:

production is understood to be a physical process, carried out under the responsibility, control and management of an institutional unit, in which labour and assets are used to transform inputs of goods and services into outputs of other goods and services. All goods and services produced as outputs must be such that they can be sold on markets or at least be capable of being provided by one unit to another, with or without charge. The SNA [system of national accounts] includes within the *production boundary* all production actually destined for the market, whether for sale or barter. It also includes all goods or services provided free to individual households or collectively to the community by government units or NPISHs [*non-profit institutions serving households*].

(United Nations 2009: 6)

Knowing this, you might still need to read this passage several times. Basically, it is saying measure and add up what you can price or imagine a price for and ignore the rest. It is a horrible technical definition because deciding what to measure, and how, is a horribly difficult question. This is partly because the accepted answers can change and partly because the economy itself changes and new issues arise.

## The story of the production boundary

Figure 3.1 shows the total system and what national accounts statisticians call the *production boundary* within it. The system could be the whole planet. This makes the diagram very similar to Figure 1.2. Here, however, the system represents the national system and everything that goes on within it. Within this system there is a narrower set of activities that fall within the production boundary. It is these that the system of national accounts rule book explains how to count. This leaves a lot of good and bad inputs and

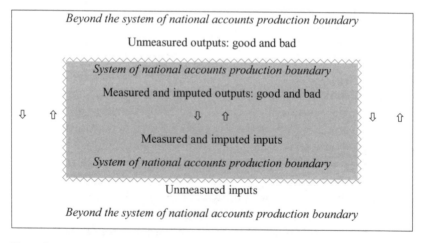

**Figure 3.1** measuring inputs and outputs: national accounts versus the real system

outputs outside the production boundary, uncounted. Within the boundary it also leads to other good and bad things being counted, perhaps inconsistently as we noted in Chapter 1.

Our diagram poses an obvious question. Is the production boundary stable over time? The answer is no: it is changing all the time. Economic development, for example, usually involves substituting buying and selling in the market for production and consumption in the home or on the farm. If this happens then activities formerly outside the production boundary will move inside. This is an example of the process of commodification: the tendency towards buying and selling everything. But it would be wrong to assume that this process only works in one direction. The production boundary can also contract because of decommodification and it can expand again because of recommodification. Water offers a simple example. When collected from streams it would not have been counted according to the logic here. Then in pre-industrial and industrial towns companies supplied water for profit. It was then partially decommodified and became a de facto free good supplied by governments (which might have been counted in a different way). Then water was not only privatized again in some economies but a large market has developed for bottled water sales, some of which is actually bottled tap water.

Water is far from unique. Quite a few things seem to move backwards and forwards. The issue that has led to most criticism about how measures of inputs and outputs are calculated is the role of the domestic or household economy. This is said to distort our understanding both of the real economy and the role of women within it. Arthur Pigou gave the classic example many years ago:

> the services rendered by women enter into the dividend when they are rendered in exchange for wages, whether in the factory or in the home, but do not enter into it when they are rendered by mothers and wives gratuitously to their own families. Thus, if a man marries his housekeeper or his cook, the national dividend is diminished.
> (Pigou 1932: 32–3)

You can see the problem with this logic. In Pigou's example marriage leads to decommodification of the woman's work and so its exclusion from the formal economic calculation. In fact domestic labour can also include quite a lot of work done by males but the argument that ignoring it devalues the contribution of women more is correct. Clearly production in the home involves some large inputs and it also has large outputs, and not least children who become workers, but none matter if they are outside the production boundary (Antonopoulos 2008; Heintz 2019).

It is not just the production of things. Care – whether in terms of bringing up children or looking after the elderly – is more often done within families. It is not counted, but it is if it is done by paid outsiders. Education is seen as something which improves the labour input and is also an output in its own right – it is counted – but that bit of our upbringing done within our families is not counted. Alvin Toffler apparently once challenged a group of business people by asking them, "how productive would your workforce be if they had not been toilet trained?" (quoted in Raworth 2018: 80). To appreciate the scale of the paradox, suppose that instead of bringing up our own child or cooking our family's dinner we each pay one another to do the other's childcare and domestic chores. Parent A looks after parent B's child for £400 a week and parent B looks after parent A's child also for £400 a week. Suddenly our cooking and childcare is now inside the production boundary and the inputs and outputs should be measured. The issues here are self-evident.

Now let us consider a second problem: do we include the informal economy within the production boundary? If I build a wall for free for you the answer is no. If you pay me to do it and I declare everything for tax the answer is yes. But what if I do it for cash and do not declare it, perhaps to escape VAT payments? My labour input and the wall as an output is now part of the grey, informal economy. The size of the informal economy varies between time and place. Crudely we can say that the less developed the economy, the bigger the role it will play. But in many parts of the world, as we noted in Chapter 1, there has also been a dramatic recent rise in the size of the informal economy. Even in very advanced economies its role is far from negligible. It is conventionally said that the informal economy in advanced societies is of the order of 10–15 per cent of the whole economy. In the transition economies of the former Soviet bloc it is 20–30 per cent and in developing economies it is 30–45 per cent. For some economies the scale of the informal economy is even higher; in Nigeria it is often said to be over 60 per cent.

It would seem logical then to include it. But since it exists below the radar, how do we measure it? The figures we have just quoted are as much guesstimates as estimates. Informal activity also presents another logical dilemma. It survives by breaking the rules. The most enthusiastic free market economists say so much the worse for the rules. But what if what happens only makes sense because standards are not followed, labour is paid a pittance and taxes not paid? Is the price at which something is then done really the measure of its true value and are inputs not properly accounted for? Could we ever really calculate a meaningful productivity figure for the informal sector? One of the easiest ways to improve the appearance of your economy is to make a bigger estimate for the size of the informal economy. This is exactly what happened in countries like Italy and Greece in the 2000s. By making the outputs look larger (inputs were more rarely adjusted) they created an inflated view of the size of their economies and also helped to distort productivity calculations.

This brings us to a third issue. The informal economy shades into the criminal or black economy and so does some of the formal economy. This is not just an issue for poor countries. London is said, by some of its critics, to be the biggest money laundering centre in the world (Persaud 2017). Dirty money goes in one end and comes out clean the other. We have to consider whether we are going to include this. A gut response might be to say no, it is criminal, so it must fall outside the production boundary. But the criminal and semi-criminal economy uses resources and has outputs, much of which involves economic transactions. What is deemed to be criminal is also an artefact of the law, and the law varies over time and between countries. Take sex and drugs. In some countries the selling of some sex and some drugs is now legal. Can we include the buying and selling of drugs in the calculations for some countries and not others? This doesn't seem to make sense, so the recent trend has been to include them by making estimates of their value for countries where their buying and selling continues to be illegal. In the case of the UK this led to the first inclusions in 2014. They allegedly added £10 billion to output. There was and is dispute about the headline figures and how they are calculated. Since you asked, the problem is to find ways of estimating the number of sex workers, the number of clients and the number of visits they make and the fees paid. Critics argue that the estimates suggest an implausibly high number of sex workers and visits or that paid-for sex is very expensive. What is asked less often is whether the inputs are being properly counted. The Labour Force Survey in the UK, for example, does not seem to include sex workers or drug dealers nor the hours these might work.

We have looked at these issues as logical ones, but they also become measurement ones. Notice that in Figure 3.1, the production boundary is drawn as a dotted line. This reflects the fact that in reality the boundary is porous. However we decide things logically, it is always possible for inputs and outputs to leach through the boundary. This will lead to things being wrongly recorded as inside the boundary, or not counted if they appear outside. There are many ways in which this can arise, but one we shall return to. This is the implication of doing paid work from home for our understanding of the labour and capital input and some aspects of output.

## The neglected problem of imputing

The problem of imputing is one of the most underdiscussed aspects of national income accounting. Imputation has been defined as "a flow that must be estimated by the national accountant because there is no directly related monetary transaction recorded by a party to the transaction". There are two major imputation adjustments made to output calculations. One is a housing adjustment which is made to reflect different consumption patterns between countries. Country A, for example, might have all owner-occupied housing. In country B housing might be all rented. The rents in country B will appear in its national accounts but there will be no rents in country A, so output will appear lower. To equalize this, an imputation adds a notional rental value for owner-occupied homes.

The second major imputation relates to what is called the FIRE sector (finance, insurance and real estate). The biggest problem here is how we measure the role of the banking sector, or to use the jargon, financial intermediation services indirectly measured (FISIM). Do financial operations create new value or transfer existing value? The answer is that in the last three decades statisticians have succumbed to pressure to change the national accounting procedure in ways that make finance appear to be a bigger positive contributor to total output. A lot of people are very unhappy about this. The problem is only partly that it takes no account of the bad things finance has done and the bailouts the sector has got. The bigger problem is that the new ways of doing the calculation inflate the importance of the sector (Mazzucato 2018a). Indeed, Jacob Assa argues that if advanced countries can now better count numbers than poor ones, the way they increase their GDPs by "financializing" them makes their figures more distorted than those of developing economies (Assa 2017).

The result is a growing disconnect between GDP as a measure and the "real" economy. This matters for us too. In 2009 Lloyd Blankfein, the CEO of Goldman Sachs, said "the people of Goldman Sachs are amongst the most productive in the world". The comment produced consternation but technically he might be right. His part of the finance sector employs relatively few people but it now seems to add enormously to value added. We get a totally illusory view of its productivity in relation to other things and overall productivity. Financialization muddies everything, including the things that matter in this book. In the UK imputed rents are now 10 per cent of GDP. The adjustments for FISIM have added at least another 5 per cent. The nervousness of those who have queried the logic of this is understandable.

Imputations raise other problems. Why do some and not others? We could hire all our clothes, but we own most of them. Should not a value be imputed for their rental? What do we do with Airbnb or house swaps for holidays? Since the statistics now include paid sex then why not impute a value for free sex? Such questions illustrate again the arbitrary nature of the conventions used to measure output and to decide what is inside and outside of the production boundary. Statisticians often respond by accepting this but saying that the subsequent adjustments would be small compared to the big adjustments the imputations make. But enormous effort is made to measure small contributions to output in other areas, so this seems little more than saying that precision in some areas but sloppiness in others is fine, and don't probe too deeply as to why.

## Do inputs equal outputs? The problem of the state

Some 35–50 per cent (and occasionally more) of GDP in advanced economies is government "spending". Part of this is called transfer spending because it uses taxes to redistribute income through the welfare state. This involves inputs to administer but no new outputs, so we would not add it to GDP. (If our measure of output were broader – say happiness – and we accept the logic of diminishing returns, then we might increase welfare by redistribution.) But other types of state activity seem to involve both inputs and outputs. States build roads; they provide defence, hospitals, schools, etc.

This raises the question of whether this activity involves the production of end goods or intermediate goods? The pioneers of national income analysis thought the answer was a bit of both and that it was necessary to distinguish between the two. But this was one of the problems that codifiers of GDP solved by fiat. They considered that the state produced end goods and not intermediate goods.

This led them to a second dilemma: how do we price the inputs and outputs of the state sector? State activity does not take place in the free market or even as semi-free market activity. There is no free market for putting a fire out in a burning building. There is no free market (or there is not supposed to be) for making nuclear weapons. The solution of the codifiers was that state activity should be valued at cost or estimated cost. Richard Stone recognized the problem this created (note what he adds together):

> This treatment, whereby commercial services are valued at market prices, government services are valued at cost, and unpaid household services are simply ignored, is not a matter of principle but practical convenience. It can be defended, therefore only on practical grounds. (Quoted in Coyle 2015: 101)

Hopefully you can see the problem this is going to create for analysing productivity in the state sector if we use value calculations. Since outputs = inputs there can be no productivity growth. This is another example of what happens when we go down the GDP rabbit hole. Clearly there has been massive real productivity growth in some aspects of what the state does. But the problem may not always be understatement. Consider for example the proliferation of inspection regimes which have emerged with the development of pseudo markets. They have added inputs but have they added any real value? However, if outputs equal inputs in the world of the figures then their results will always be neutral.

## More price–value problems

We have seen that economists like to think that prices are a measure of values. To compare computer output over time we calculate the total number of computers produced times their price. But a computer today is not only cheaper than one in the past, it is much better in almost every respect. So, would such a calculation capture the huge quality improvements that have been made? If it doesn't, we will understate any productivity growth. This is clearly an important issue, but how important? Some people argue that part of the explanation of any productivity slowdown today is our failure to fully capture quality improvements in our data. The slowdown would disappear if we recognized that price does not always capture quality. There is a technical solution to this problem. This is to create what is called a hedonic index in which an allowance is made for quality changes.

The bigger problem is that you cannot just change bits of your data. Statistical series need to be consistent. There is nothing unusual about quality improvements in today's goods. We saw in Chapter 2 that all technologies improve over time and that the cumulative gains can be huge. It is not obvious that modern statistics have more of a problem in capturing such quality changes than those in the past. Hedonic pricing was first suggested in the 1930s when economists noticed the enormous improvements in the motor car and wondered if car prices fully captured this.

We also depend on an ever-growing number of intangible goods. But the price–value for intangibles is complex too. Take knowledge: economists entertain contradictory views; they build models which require everyone to have perfect knowledge, but believe in a real system where knowledge can be privately owned and bought and sold. Different types of intangibles can become mixed up in products. The computer software might be proprietary and costed but the operating system might be the freely constructed Linux one. How do we price–value things like ideas, art, culture and entertainment? In what ways should Wikipedia figure in our calculations of outputs and inputs? The complexities get weirder if we try to price something like brands. The prices of all such things are often artefacts of legal systems which protect knowledge rights through patents and copyright legislation. Some argue these are simple forms of rent seeking. Their legal forms are relatively new and vary over time and place. Their "internal logic" is questionable – why is the life of a patent shorter than that of copyright, for example?

The price of a good should equal the marginal cost of its production, but some intangible goods are almost free to reproduce. There is speculation that this might be becoming true of some tangible ones too. What happens if we move towards a zero marginal cost economy? Contrary to what is sometimes claimed we cannot have a weightless economy. The infrastructures on which free knowledge depends have costs. Even libraries have to be paid for. The closer we get to a zero marginal cost then the more the "state" would have to take over infrastructure costs. But if things do become more freely available, do they cease to have economic value? These possibilities play havoc with the economic system and our ways of measuring it.

## Fiddling the books?

Statisticians come under pressure from politicians to cook "national books". Governments like the figures to look good for internal and external prestige. Yet sometimes it can be useful to make things look worse. It might get you more aid, for example. Population figures are sometimes politically contested, especially if they form the basis for the internal distribution of resources. Ironically though, the fiddling in the state sector is usually more identifiable than that which goes on in the private and semi-private sectors.

How do the accounting illusions involved in tax dodging, cheating and lying affect productivity calculations? Tax havens go back a century but their role has increased enormously. Some are "paradise islands": the Caymans or the Virgin Islands for example. A good number are UK dependencies. Big economies can be tax havens too: Ireland, the Netherlands, some even think the UK is. Tax havens can also exist *within* big economies: Delaware in the US, for example, functions to some extent this way. Tax havens perform two functions. They are "secrecy jurisdictions"; they limit what we can know about companies by having their activities formally registered overseas. And they are places to which profits can be reassigned and to which the ownership of assets may be formally shifted. Instead of activity appearing in economy A, legal accounting tricks allow it to appear in economy B or even move through economy B to economy C. The OECD calls this "base erosion" to reflect the fact that in some countries the economic tax base appears to be narrowing. In reality nothing much actually moves but a new brass plaque is put on an obscure building which is deemed to be the formal headquarters of a global giant. At the time of writing the formal headquarters of IKEA is not in Sweden but in part of a small building behind Leiden station in the Netherlands and Amazon EU is based in a back street in Luxemburg.

Big companies can bend the rules to their favour and a lot is hidden in their books, which the tax authorities struggle to see. The simplest accounting illusion is transfer pricing in intra-company transactions. A product or part produced in country A is deliberately underpriced, perhaps even seemingly made at a loss. It is then "sold" to another part of the company in another country where it is recorded at its real price. The result is that profit appears to move from A to B, distorting our basic measurements. The same trick can be played by charging a subsidiary for the right to use intellectual property whose ownership is supposedly based in another economy. Some think that the accounting illusions are so complex that some value leaves one place but never arrives in another. Such accounting illusions mean that outputs, and possibly inputs, will be reduced in some places and increased in others, creating more illusions of outputs and inputs. Variations in productivity will then have even less relation to the real situation.

## Measuring inputs

Labour productivity measured as output per hour worked is one of the best and least controversial indicators that we have in terms of measurement and logical problems. That does not mean that measuring the labour input is without difficulties. There is a quantity problem. In productivity calculations we imagine a clear separation between paid and unpaid work. We leave home and go to work. We may even be recorded in and out of our workplace. Some jobs also require people to work "officially" extra unrecorded hours at work: junior doctors in the UK are an example. The situation is worse in more poorly regulated economies. In China the law sets a 40-hour week with eight hours a day and no more than 36 hours a month overtime. Yet Jack Ma, founder of Alibaba, said, "If you join Alibaba, you should get ready to work 12 hours a day. Otherwise why did you come to Alibaba? We don't need those who comfortably work 8 hours" (*The Guardian*, 16 April 2019).

Many jobs require (allow) people to take their work home. "My job is no longer about children. It's just a 60-hour week with pressure to push children's achievement data through", said one British teacher in 2019 (*The Guardian*, 16 April 2019). Too many of us check and reply to work e-mails outside work hours. This too is an additional unrecorded labour input (and, if you think about it, a capital one). The work/non-work boundary was weak when paid work was done in cottage industries. It then seemed to grow firmer. But self-employment has grown again. In the UK, 15 per cent of the labour force is now said to be self-employed. The boundary has weakened too for white-collar workers. Put these things together and a good case can be made that the inputs of unmeasured hours have been growing and so labour productivity has been overstated.

There is an interesting question too about when work begins. If we were to include commuting time in a calculation of labour productivity it could have a significant effect not only in the very long term but also the shorter term. In Britain, the Labour Force Survey shows that the average commute length (both ways) rose from 53 minutes in 2006 to 58 minutes by 2016, an increase of nearly 10 per cent in a decade. And it was much longer in London, at 81 minutes. In 2016, commuting amounted to roughly 27 working days a year. This would be the equivalent of some 10 per cent of the labour input if it were added (*TUC News*, 17 November 2017). We might also think about people who have to wait for work. A taxi driver's real hours should be included as part of the labour input, but what of the waiting hours of a worker on the different types of zero hours contracts?

What about quality differences in the labour input? Workers have become healthier and more educated. Different workers have different levels of skill. Economists very quickly realized that it might make sense to adjust the labour input to reflect a quality element. One way of doing this is to assume that what workers get paid is what they contribute. Your wage is, in more technical terms, your marginal product. So if a worker with more education gets paid more than a worker with less education, then the pay difference reflects the contribution made by the additional education. In this type of analysis there is no discussion of power, status, bargaining, credentialization or rent extraction. No attempt is made to deal with the abundant evidence of discrimination by race and gender in the labour market. You would have to be pretty blinkered to believe that what workers get paid is a measure of what they put in. Yet when it comes to productivity calculations most economists are happy to wear these blinkers. Down the rabbit hole, bankers contribute more than those who build and maintain our sewage system.

The complications of measuring the labour input, however, are as nothing compared to those which arise when we measure the capital input. Capital is harder to define than might be imagined. The concept has been muddied by talk of human capital and natural capital. For us, capital is the infrastructures, buildings and equipment: the product of past labour that we use to assist us in our present work. But does it include the room in my house if I work from home? If it is a computer then is it the software on it too? Is intellectual capital a real thing? Should we include things like research and development in our measures of capital? A few years ago, the answer to this last question was no. Now the answer is yes, although not everyone is happy with the consequences (de Haan & Haynes 2018).

Once we have decided what capital is, we then have to calculate and *value* the capital stock. This is a huge practical problem. If we can solve it we can divide the value of the capital stock into total output. This would give us what is called the capital–output ratio. As a statistic it is very crude: it is the capital equivalent of measuring labour productivity by dividing total output by total population. If we are getting more output per unit of capital stock, that would be a rough indication that the productivity of capital is rising. But just as we really want to know output per hour worked, so for capital we need output in relation to capital used up in production. The simplest way to think about this is depreciation. Depreciation is usually thought of as the measure of the "using up" of capital. Here we hit another major difficulty. Remember the argument in Chapter 2 that real productivity growth is embodied in capital of different ages or vintages? Different types of capital will have different rates of depreciation, for example computer software might be valueless in a couple of years. Other types of capital seem to go on and on. In some places we are still using infrastructure built centuries ago. When capital is written off it seems to disappear from the statistics, but it is still there as part of the real capital stock. So this aspect also turns out to be a major problem. How is a statistical office, a group of economists, not to mention a lone one, to calculate with any sort of accuracy the depreciation of all the different types of assets in an economy?

Can we put together the different factors of production and calculate "total factor productivity"? In Lewis Carroll's stories about Alice she learned to expect things to get "Curiouser and curiouser!" Yet she still told the Red Queen that she could not "believe impossible things". The Queen replied that Alice needed more practice. "Sometimes", said the Queen, "I've believed as many as six impossible things before breakfast". To believe in calculations of total factor productivity we need to be a bit like the Red Queen.

## Total factor productivity

Much of the economic discussion of national productivity patterns is dominated by data on total factor productivity. To calculate them we need to specify a production function (Hulten 2001). We have already encountered a simple one.:

Total factor productivity growth = output change – (capital input change × capital share) – (labour input change × labour share)

To make the idea work we need to choose what type of production function we are going to use because there are different ones. But whichever we choose we will have to accept some very strange things.

First, we will have to believe in a number of logical impossibilities. Production functions tend to assume perfectly competitive economies. No economy meets these conditions. And there are hidden assumptions too that stretch credulity. Constant returns to scale is one, perfect substitutability of factors is another.

Second, we are going to have to accept what some see as weighting impossibilities. To add together capital and labour we know we have to find a way of weighing their contributions. At this point economists divide into hostile camps. In the late nineteenth century, the founding fathers of neoclassical economics noticed that in the perfect competition model the marginal products of labour, land and capital had to be proportional to their earnings. John Bates Clark invested this idea with a moral force: "What a social class gets is, under natural law, what it contributes to the general output of industry" (Clark 1891: 313). There is no exploitation in capitalism, merely a fair and logical set of rewards that reflect relative contributions. An economic logic determines more or less fixed relative shares (often said to result in a one-third share to profit and two-thirds share to labour). Neoclassical economists see the world in terms of:

Output = profits + wages

Those who are critical of neoclassical economics tear their hair out at this. They argue that labour–capital shares can just as easily be seen as the outcome of distributional struggles, and that they are therefore no guide to real contributions and productivity. If capital is strengthened then the wages share goes down, and if labour is strengthened the capital share goes down. Certainly over time, and between countries, there are important variations in the relative shares going to profit and wages that seem to make little sense in terms of a marginal theory of distribution and by implication productivity. In recent decades one of the biggest problems has been the fall in the wage share (Piketty 2014). Warren Buffett, the US billionaire, said with commendable honesty, "There's class warfare, all right, but it's my class, the rich class, that's making war, and we're winning."

Many "bosses" effectively set their own pay levels. One of the most astonishing shifts of the last decades had been the explosion of high pay and extraordinary pay differentials at the top of companies. In the UK, for example, the mean ratio of FTSE 100 CEO pay exploded from 20 times the average worker's pay to 130 times in 2016. To seek to explain this using a marginal productivity theory would seem absurd, all the more so since the pattern seems to bear no relation to company performance (Peston 2017: 48–9, 186–7).

Our third impossibility, to which we have already referred in Chapter 2, is the disembodiment impossibility. If we take the total factor productivity calculations seriously then their logic seems to be that capital formation doesn't matter much. At best it accounts for 10–15 per cent of output growth.

Our fourth impossible is the impossible residual. We have already seen that the production function does not really measure productivity at all. Total factor productivity is what is left after we have done our calculations of the imagined contributions of the inputs. It is a residual, sometimes referred to as the measure of our ignorance. It includes what we don't know and all the mistakes that arise in the process of dealing with the issues we have discussed so far. It is an error term. If we undercount inputs then this will magnify the apparent residual. Attempts are also made to try to decompose this residual element into what we imagine are its components. But suppose we could do this: the more we explain by the input side, the less we are left with on the output side. Adjusting our inputs to take account of their improving quality, for example, appears to reduce total factor productivity. Zvi Griliches once suggested that if full account were taken of all the adjustments we could make then not only might technological change disappear, it might even become negative, which is about as bizarre a result as we might imagine.

For some the analysis of total factor productivity is the height of sophistication. For others it is little more than alchemy. Meaningful discussions of productivity can better use indicators like output per hour worked, so we are far from reliant on total factor productivity. These indicators have their problems too, but they make fewer "impossible" demands on our credulity.

**4**

# Can productivity growth go on forever?

Many of our news stories seem to be about global warming, pollution, species loss and protests about the threat of global extinction. These stories arise from a fear that the system that has given us productivity growth is out of control. There are also stories about continuing productivity problems in different economies, not least the UK. These stories assume that we have to find a way to get even more productivity growth. This chapter is about this contradiction and the question of whether productivity growth can go on forever. In the first part we ask can the planet support unlimited productivity growth? This question necessarily challenges the narrow view that many economists hold of the economic system. In the second part we accept, for the sake of argument, this narrower view but ask to what extent is productivity growth in advanced capitalism already slowing down and could we reverse it if we wanted to?

## Productivity and planetary possibilities

The economist Kenneth Boulding is supposed to have said, "anyone who believes exponential growth can go on forever in a finite world is either a madman or an economist". The normal laws of physics are not suspended in economics, but when conventional economists look to the future they tend to ignore these laws. They have the implicit, sometimes explicit, view that the economy is some kind of perpetual motion machine that can go on getting bigger forever.

Some people think about this problem in terms of population. We know that the magic of productivity growth has enabled the world's population to grow. But the problem is not really the number of people. In fact, the rate of the world's population growth has been slowing since the early 1960s.

Absolute numbers are still rising, so in the next decades the world's population will peak, perhaps at around 10 billion. Numbers will then start to fall. Birth rates have been falling sharply for a long time and, in some places, they are already below replacement levels (Dorling 2013).

The problem is that we all want the same high standard of living and to maintain it. Table 4.1 shows estimates of the numbers of people who have ever lived and the share of all the output they have produced and consumed during the time they were and are alive. The 5 billion born between 1950 and 1995 will have produced just under 30 per cent of all the output produced by all humans before they die, and the 3 billion born since 1995 just under another 30 per cent. These are rough calculations made on the basis of the estimated number of humans born in period x and their estimated life expectancy multiplied by estimated annual output per head. Much depends on the assumptions. The estimated numbers of humans born before 1750 is the most controversial. Some think it much too high. If so then the share of output produced by those born in more recent times increases even more. Either way, we can easily see how production and consumption have speeded up. But, of course, we produce and consume unequally. Most of this production and consumption has been done in those economies with the highest levels of per capita income and the highest levels of productivity. Within them it is the richest people and most powerful organizations who are the biggest problem. Some 75 per cent of climate change is attributable to the operations of just 100 state and private "carbon corporations" (CDP UK 2017). Yet we are offered a perspective in which we can both keep increasing productivity forever and the less productive can become more productive by catching up through more of the same.

**Table 4.1** Estimates of all humans born and share of total human output produced during their lifetimes

| | Billion born in period | % of all humans born | % of all output produced by humans in lifespan |
|---|---|---|---|
| 50,000 BCE–1750 CE | 90 | 83 | 27 |
| 1750–1950 | 10 | 9 | 15 |
| 1950–95 | 5 | 5 | 28 |
| 1995–2017 | 3 | 3 | 29 |

Source: Author's estimates based on Population Reference Bureau estimates and Maddison data.

Suppose for a minute that poor countries could do this. Catching up by growing faster means chasing impossible levels of income and wealth for the whole world at the catch-up point. We can see this in the estimates of what it would mean for world output. We can see it too in the estimates for individual goods. In 1976, the number of cars and trucks in the world was 342 million. In 1996 it was 670 million and by 2016 some 1.32 billion. If all the world's countries were rich enough to have the same number of cars per head as in the UK today that would be nearly 5 billion cars – an increase of 3–4 times. Do the calculation on the US figure and you get 7 billion. Factor in growth and future global figures get even higher.

This is the distorted logic of exponential growth. The consequences of how we have achieved past productivity growth are already putting enormous pressure on our world. Yet economists are still reluctant to face up to the simple fact that we cannot have infinite expansion on a finite planet.

The earth has existed for some 14–15 billion years. Life on it for 5 billion. Every form of life interacts with the planet in some way. Usually the inter-action is modest. This has not stopped a series of extinction events, defined as 75 per cent species loss in a short period. The last – perhaps caused by a meteor hit – led to the elimination of the dinosaurs and many of the species of their time. For much of the human era, we have had a significant but more modest and protracted impact. This changed with the development of cap-italism and in particular the intensification of agriculture, industrialization and the rise of cities. These processes both reflected productivity growth and helped to drive it on, but they also created growing physical demands on the planet.

As the economic system has grown so the background extinction rate – the rate at which species disappear – increased. Moreover, there is worry that these pressures are not linear or a straight line on a graph: there can be tipping points where change accelerates and becomes irreversible. The fear of a possible global warming tipping point is an example of what a nonlinear threat might look like.

To see why these problems exist we need to go back to Figure 1.2, which pictured the economy as part of a bigger set of closed planetary processes. Conventional economics is about the buying and selling of commodities and the efficiency with which this is done. But economic systems are also part of physical systems and cannot escape their physical laws.

## Fantasy economics and economic "madmen"

One way to measure the overall impact of these physical problems is to consider the planetary footprint that the economic system creates. If the planetary footprint is 1.0 or less then we are working within the planet's capacity. The system will probably be more or less sustainable. If the footprint is more than 1.0 then we are using up resources and creating problems faster than one planet can support. Table 4.2 shows the equivalent global planetary footprints if the whole world were to consume at the levels of the countries concerned. The bigger the number, the bigger the number of equivalent planets we would need if these national consumption levels were generalized. Some question the data but they are improving over time and the picture is clear.

**Table 4.2** Global planetary footprint, assuming the whole planet consumed at specified country-year levels

|      | World | US   | UK   | Europe | Japan | China | Africa |
|------|-------|------|------|--------|-------|-------|--------|
| 1961 | 0.73  | 2.58 | 1.97 | 1.29   | 0.98  | 0.31  | 0.40   |
| 1970 | 1.01  | 3.87 | 2.61 | 2.07   | 1.89  | 0.40  | 0.51   |
| 1980 | 1.19  | 4.24 | 2.48 | 2.49   | 2.13  | 0.58  | 0.65   |
| 1990 | 1.29  | 4.78 | 2.81 | 2.71   | 2.69  | 0.75  | 0.67   |
| 2000 | 1.37  | 5.47 | 3.07 | 2.63   | 2.89  | 1.04  | 0.71   |
| 2010 | 1.66  | 5.17 | 3.13 | 2.91   | 2.76  | 1.98  | 0.82   |
| 2014 | 1.69  | 4.97 | 2.85 | 2.79   | 2.82  | 2.21  | 0.82   |

*Source*: https://www.footprintnetwork.org/.

We see that in the 1970s the world went into ecological deficit. Today the global footprint for the planet as a whole is nearly two planets. We also see that the most advanced countries have long been in ecological deficit. In recent decades the planetary ecological pressure of these advanced countries has fallen somewhat: partly because of ecological improvements, partly because they have exported their dirty processes elsewhere (although the pressures remain) and partly because of the economic slowdown. But if the whole world consumed at the current US level, we would need the equivalent of nearly five planets. And when growth occurs, driven by productivity change as it has in China, then the ecological costs rise too. Today only Africa is in ecological surplus, but that is because it is still poor. It looks impossible to solve these problems by simply imagining that we can do more of the same.

Thinking in terms of these bigger processes raises three issues: the resource demand problem, the way we convert inputs into outputs and the output problem. Table 4.3 sets out these three elements.

How does this affect the possibilities of productivity growth? Physical resource inputs are all finite but some are more abundant than others. They are unequally distributed across the globe and are treated as local assets whose use is controlled by individuals, corporations and states. Even if abundant somewhere on the planet, there may still be problems and costs of access in other parts. The technology of extraction has everywhere improved, but as the use of these resources has intensified so too has the difficulty of extraction. Oil when first used bubbled freely to the surface, then it was extracted from wells, now some of it is accessed through fracking. These problems are compounded if there are negative feedback mechanisms. Efficiency gains can improve what is extracted from the resources we

**Table 4.3** Throughput in the economy as a total system

| Resource inputs | Illusory high-productivity conversions? | "Waste" outputs |
| --- | --- | --- |
| Fossil fuels | Economic productivity | Global warming |
| Minerals (including 17 rare | OR | Deforestation |
| earth ones) | Economic/energy | Desertification |
| Oceans | productivity | Air pollution |
| Fresh water | OR | Ocean acidification |
| Cultivable land | Total energy productivity | Habitat loss |
| Biomass | | Species loss |
| Air | | |

**Table 4.4** The rise in global fuel consumption by type, 1960–2017

| | Million tons oil equivalent | Index | % from | | |
| --- | --- | --- | --- | --- | --- |
| | | | Fossil | Nuclear | Renewable |
| 1960 | 3,701 | 100 | 94.7 | 0.2 | 5.7 |
| 2000 | 9,356 | 253 | 86.9 | 6.2 | 6.9 |
| 2010 | 12,119 | 327 | 87.1 | 5.3 | 7.6 |
| 2017 | 13,511 | 365 | 85.2 | 4.4 | 10.4 |

*Source*: BP Statistical Review of World Energy database.

input, but in the real world, for output to increase there has to be an increase in inputs. This is crucially the case with energy. Table 4.4 shows how energy use has increased. Although there has been some switch to renewables, the greater part of the increase in energy consumption has come from fossil fuels. It is difficult to imagine, therefore, the pressure on resources in general, and energy in particular, stabilizing or declining unless demand is also stabilized or declines.

The same applies to the unwanted outputs. The last column in Table 4.3. shows these. The most obvious today are greenhouse gases. The earth is estimated to be hotter than at any time in the last 800,000 years. The amount of $CO_2$ in the atmosphere has increased by 30 per cent since 1770 and methane by 140 per cent. Some of it is absorbed, but an important part of the greenhouse gas emissions is accumulated and it is this accumulation and the continuing high levels of greenhouse gas production that threaten to be so catastrophic.

Economists often respond to these arguments by arguing that they can be solved by increasing the productivity of resource use – getting more from less and producing less waste in the process. Yet too often they focus on the immediate impact of technological change and not on the total process. If a new gas heater increases the efficiency with which it produces heat, this looks positive. But we need to look at the efficiency of total inputs and outputs, the production of the heater, the gas in relation to the heat output and so on. Despite their claim to understand how the global economy is linked together, economists often have a poor grasp of the total processes involved (Raynes & Nair 1984, is still a valuable explanation of this failing).

We need to analyse the economy as a total system of inputs and outputs. This idea was pioneered by economists, but attempts are now being made to expand this idea by looking at the total "burden" that production and consumption place on the planetary system in terms of energy, carbon footprints, etc. We saw in Chapter 1, for example, the significant gains made in terms of agricultural productivity. But if we think in terms of energy throughput the picture is rather different. The estimate is that every energy calorie that cattle produce in terms of meat or dairy requires an input of eight or nine calories. The total energy productivity is therefore very poor – even if we ignore the unwanted wastes. Pour milk and sugar on a processed breakfast cereal and the energy efficiency of what is in the bowl diminishes even more. The idea of the dematerialization of the economy takes on a

## BOX 4.1. ENERGY PRODUCTIVITY: A DIFFERENT TYPE OF MEASURE?

Energy productivity is often thought of in terms of GDP or value added per final energy input: measured, for example, in terms of barrel of oil equivalent.

$$\frac{\text{GDP/value added}}{\text{Final energy consumption}}$$

We divide output by final energy consumption because we want to know all the energy that goes into making the product. Think of breakfast cereal. We need to know the energy consumed in the production (and distribution) of the cereal and the packaging, from the start of the process to final consumption. (We should even include dealing with the waste.) This is a useful measure of energy productivity but it is still only partial. It assumes for the numerator that price = value.

Now consider the idea that what is involved is an energy conversion in which energy goes in and energy comes out. Then we would calculate:

$$\frac{\text{Final energy output}}{\text{Final energy input}}$$

The problem is that it is basic science that we always get less out than we put in. This calculation allows us to see how much. Now the breakfast cereal looks an even worse deal not only because the contents require so much energy to produce but so does the packaging and distribution. We get a relatively small food energy value out. One estimate is one calorie embodied in a cornflake takes seven calories of energy input to produce. Maximizing energy productivity in these terms is very different from maximizing GDP output per unit of input.

We can also think about an even more negative productivity calculation directly related to global warming. We could measure the amount of $CO_2$ equivalent produced for every unit of output, measured in either price or physical terms. For example:

$$\frac{\text{Final } CO_2e \text{ produced}}{\text{e.g. £ output}} \quad \text{or} \quad \frac{\text{Final } CO_2e \text{ produced}}{\text{e.g. Transport mile by type}}$$

different perspective when it is realized that the carbon footprint of an Apple Mac – before it is used – is the same as a journey by air of over 2,000 miles, or that the world's global data centres consume 2 per cent of the world's electricity production and produce the same amount of $CO_2$ as the global airline industry (Jones 2018).

Some economists get around this problem by building tricks into their models. One trick is to imagine that capital and labour can be substituted for resources. Herman Daly has suggested that this is rather like thinking that you can bake the same size cake if you use half the flour but two cake makers instead of one (Daly 2007). It also ignores the fact that capital and labour themselves need resources to produce. Another trick is to suggest that what William Nordhaus called "backstop technologies" will be found (Nordhaus 1973). These are imagined future "optimal, efficient technologies" that will magically resolve problems. This allows economists to have faith that we can go on as before. It diverts attention from the argument that technological change within capitalism is biased towards perpetuating the system as it is. The future "techno fix" argument also blinds us both to the possibility that the technologies already exist or substantial parts of them do to reduce the loading. The problem might really be that, as the system is currently configured, there is a limited incentive to use them.

There is another issue. In the nineteenth century, Stanley Jevons realized that as the efficiency of coal use improved so demand for coal rose instead of falling. "It is wholly a confusion of ideas to suppose that the economical use of fuel is equivalent to a diminished consumption. The very contrary is the truth", he wrote (Jevons 1906 [1865]: 140). This has since been known as the Jevons paradox and it is not difficult to find modern examples. The extraordinary increase in the efficiency of lighting has led to us putting lights everywhere. Fuel efficiency in cars has led to more use and new demands through innovations like air conditioning. Resolving any Jevons paradox takes us back not to another techno fix but to the way the economy is organized.

Many economists still reject this. Instead of seeing the economic system as a subsystem of a planetary one, they try to analyse the planetary system as a subsystem of the economic one. "Nature" in all its forms becomes "natural capital". Its use, and misuse, can then be priced and seemingly internalized into economic analysis in general and productivity analysis in particular. In the UK, for example, the government in 2012 established a natural capital committee under Dieter Helm who endorsed the view that "the environment is part of the economy and needs to be properly integrated into it so that growth opportunities will not be missed" (quoted in Simms 2016). In 2019, Partha Dasgupta was appointed to report in very similar terms on the economic case for biodiversity. To its critics this looked like another example of an "economics imperialism" in which "economics" as a subject and the economic subsystem as a thing seeks to subordinate more and more of life and the ecosphere to its narrow calculus.

## The productivity frontier and the rest

Now the second big question. Within the narrow confines of the economic system as it is normally theorized, is productivity growth already falling? Even in the very early stages of more rapid productivity growth, in the first part of the nineteenth century, economists began to worry that capitalism might eventually lose its dynamism and move towards a stationary state. Today the performance of the most advanced economies seems anaemic. How do we make sense of this?

We can begin by making an important distinction between different types of growth and productivity change in the global economy. The states that make up the world economy are, in economic terms, strung out with huge gaps between the least developed and the most developed, as in Figure 4.1.

The overall growth of the world economy, and productivity change within it, will reflect the experience of all of these economies. The economic history of capitalism is partly the story of its expansion outwards from an inner core

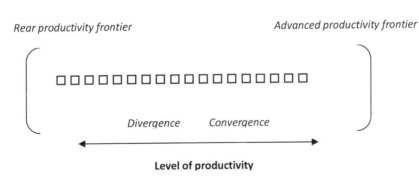

**Figure 4.1** Three forms of productivity advance in the global economy

into the whole world. This is what we mean by the movement of the *rear productivity frontier*. In our view, expansion by integration was effectively completed in the late nineteenth century and early twentieth centuries, but some argue that what David Harvey has called "accumulation by dispossession" is still continuing (Harvey 2004). Once integrated, the productivity levels of national economies can then either *converge* on or *diverge* from those of the most advanced economies, a problem we will look at in Chapters 5–7. The most advanced part of the system is that defined by the *advanced productivity frontier*. Productivity here has to grow more slowly. Pushing *out* the production frontier, we know, involves finding new ways of doing new things. This is not as easy as copying proven technologies and methods.

While catch-up economies can make quick productivity gains, at the frontier long-run productivity growth, represented by that of the US, has for a century or more tended to average around 1–2 per cent per year. This long-run figure is not stable. Figure 4.2 shows one measure of labour productivity for four leading economies for the last half century. We use labour productivity partly to avoid the issues of total factor productivity measurement, but also because the data are available on an annual basis. Three

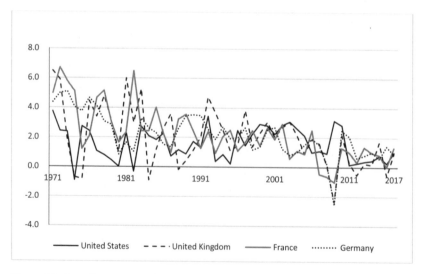

**Figure 4.2** Annual percentage change in GDP (in constant prices) per hour worked for 4 leading economies

*Source*: OECD.

things are immediately apparent. The first is that it looks as if there is some convergence in the rates of productivity change over time between the four countries. A second is the great short-term variation in the rates of productivity growth. A third is that it looks very much as if there is a declining trend over time. We shall look in more detail at the issue of the convergence in productivity rates between advanced countries in Chapter 5. Here let us concentrate on the second and third points.

## Productivity and the economic cycle

We can track shorter-term variations of productivity growth in annual and seasonal cycles. But most attention has been paid to longer-term business cycles which last several years and that, as the global economy has become more integrated, have also become linked internationally. The early economists recognized that there were booms and slumps but thought they were the product of external factors: the weather affected the harvest, wars and political events caused disruption. It was Marx who focused on the way that these cycles were intrinsic to capitalism and developed an analysis in which, Schumpeter later said, "we find practically all the elements that ever entered into any serious analysis of business cycles, and on the whole very little error" (Schumpeter 1976 [1943]: 40). But after 1945, macroeconomic analysis and macroeconomic policy tended to see them as fluctuations around an equilibrium path. Some economists agreed with Paul Samuelson in his textbook assertion that as a result of government policy, "the wild business cycle that ravaged mature capitalism during its early years has been tamed". Others thought it had disappeared naturally. The "central problem of depression-prevention [has] been solved, for all practical purposes", Robert Lucas said in 2003 (Lucas 2003: 1). That seemed optimistic then. It looks foolish now.

The problem is to know whether productivity growth is pro- or counter-cyclical. If it is pro-cyclical then productivity will go down when the economy goes down and go up when the economy goes up. This appears to be the case. The underlying determinants of productivity, investment and expenditure on research and development tend to be pro-cyclical. As an economy goes down, excess capacity will also develop. This will be all the more so if labour is hoarded and less productive capital kept in use because companies are expecting better times or have subsidies of one kind or another. When the economy turns up more capacity is used and the rate of investment and technical change increases. When we look at firms though, it seems likely that those that cut back in major ways during depressions are unlikely to gain a new wind in expansions: productivity growth is more likely to be driven by new entrants who also encourage the process of structural change (Bhaumik 2011).

## The possibility of stagnation

Figure 4.2 pointed to a long-term slowing of the rate of productivity growth. Are there then longer-term variations in the rate of expansion and productivity growth at the frontier? Might there be an internal, endogenous pattern that persists over a number of business cycles and which could, over time, cause the system to slow down, perhaps even driving it towards stagnation? Figure 4.3 supplements Figure 4.2 with long-run data which give us some idea of how the rate of growth at the frontier has changed and, behind it, of the shifts in the measured rate of productivity growth for the US and the Euro-15. Although we can do much more complex forms of analysis it seems clear that here there is no steady long-term equilibrium path.

Given that there are shorter-term economic cycles it is natural to ask if there might be a longer-term "super" cycle? In the 1920s the Russian economist Nikolai Kondratiev speculated that there might be a deeper pattern to capitalist expansion. He focused more on price swings. It was Schumpeter who gave the argument for long cycles more form by arguing that they arose because of a tendency of invention and innovation to cluster at some points in history. Few followed him, but when the postwar boom ended in the 1970s there was a renewed interest, at least among more heterodox commentators. Mainstream economists of the time like Paul Samuelson were dismissive of the attempted resurrection of "Kondratiev moonshine". Another half century on and some still see "moonshine" where others see a regularity. There are two obvious difficulties with this view. The first is whether any longer-term variations can actually be measured as "cyclical phenomena" rather than shifts (possibly ad hoc) in the long-term trend. The second is whether the pattern – whatever it is – can be satisfactorily explained by some cyclical mechanism internal to capitalism.

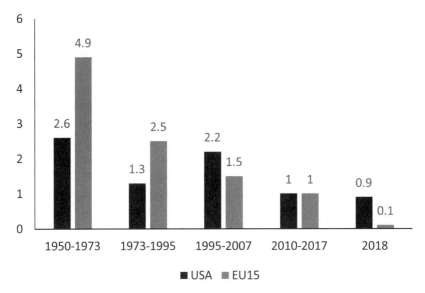

**Figure 4.3** Percentage annual growth of GDP per hour worked for US and Euro-15, 1950–2018

*Source*: Earlier data from Crafts (2017). Later data from The Conference Board. The figure for the later Euro-15 is an unweighted average of Austria, Belgium, Denmark, Finland, France, Germany, Luxemburg, Netherlands, Portugal, Spain, Sweden and the UK.

If there are no super-cycles then could we be seeing something different, a trend switch and a "secular tendency to stagnation"?

## Keep calm and carry on?

From the perspective outlined at the start of this chapter a productivity growth slowdown, if real, might be welcomed. But this tends not to be the view of mainstream economists. Some, however, do argue that there is nothing to worry about. One group argues that any slowdown is an illusion: an artefact of the data. We saw in the last chapter how big a problem productivity measurement is. Some accounts now argue that the output figure fails to capture the true scale of improvements in quality and the availability of free goods, etc., especially associated with things such as computers, smartphones and social networks. But we also know that such quality measurement problems go back a long way. It is not clear that the changes that might not be captured in the statistics today are greater. Nor from a shorter-term perspective is it plausible to argue that in relation to the digital economy they have become larger in the last decade than say the 1990s. The size of the digital sector is just not big enough to explain the much bigger declines in the data. There is no real correlation between the measured declines in productivity and the size of IT sectors within or between economies. Real economic performance in some of the most high-profile new technology pales in comparison to stock market valuations and media hype (Syverson 2017). It is striking too how keen some economists are to argue that the data understate gains. If we return to Figure 4.3, we see that in the early 2000s productivity was pulled upwards for a time in the United States. Without this the trend rate would be even worse. But was this increase itself real or might it have been inflated by "socially useless activity" in a bubble economy? The numbers argument can work both ways.

A second argument that is dismissive of the possibility of a longer-run slowdown focuses on the issue of implementation lags. This is an application of the argument about general purpose technologies and the time it takes for their impact to be felt. As with older technologies, so the realization of the possibilities of computers, artificial intelligence and machine learning will need to be spread across sectors and developed in depth. It will require as yet undeveloped complementary technologies and organizational forms. In one version it is even suggested that the sky-high valuations of "new technology firms", rather than being driven upwards by the herd instinct of investors, actually reflects the financial markets' better understanding of the real future potential of new technology (Brynjolfsson *et al.* 2017).

A third argument which suggests a limited cause for concern is that we may be seeing an intensification of Baumol's cost disease, noted in Chapter 2. Remember that this is the argument that rich societies will eventually move more and more resources into sectors where labour-saving gains are limited. Is this a "disease"? "Disease" theorists say yes. They look to cure it by mechanizing or computerizing previously "one-to-one" jobs. In 2018, software developed by PricewaterhouseCoopers was said to be able to review contracts at 30 times the speed of a human and at one-eighth the cost. And who needs teachers when you can take a MOOC: a massive open on-line course? Others are more sanguine. A key part of the argument for productivity growth is that it provides us with the basis of both more leisure and better human relationships. In these terms the issue is not so much "Baumol's disease" as the failure to take advantage of Baumol's "opportunity". Instead of using the possibilities created by high productivity, we increase the number of unproductive "bullshit" jobs (Graeber 2018). We create ever-lengthening data requirements, form filling and levels of monitoring. And when the jobs are necessary, we reward them poorly. Many person-to-person jobs are poorly paid, and even many live performers – including Baumol's musicians – struggle to make a good living. These are big issues and we will return to them in Chapter 8.

Here we need to turn to those who take the threat of a deeper-rooted productivity slowdown more seriously.

## Stagnation theories

The possibility of secular stagnation has been argued to arise from a number of sources. In most scenarios slowing productivity growth has not been seen as a direct cause of a wider slowdown in growth but an indirect consequence of other factors which have reduced, or are reducing, the dynamism of advanced economies. Indeed, when Alvin Hansen developed the idea of secular stagnation in the late 1930s, he thought it compatible with increasing productivity. Having argued that the overall dynamism of the American economy had been reduced by the ending of internal expansion to the West and slowing population growth, he then, after the 1937 economic crisis had cut short the recovery from the 1929 one, added in a Keynesian element to his arguments. Increasing productivity was contributing to surplus capacity in the economy and unemployment. Today, however, what strikes those who think we are faced with a degree of secular stagnation is the combination of sluggish economic growth *and* sluggish productivity growth.

One approach to secular stagnation does see slowing productivity growth as a significant direct factor in slowing economic growth overall. This is a "supply side" view in which technological change is determined largely exogenously, outside of the economic system narrowly defined. Those who support this view tend to be pessimistic about the possibility of increasing the trend of productivity growth in the future. This view is especially associated with the work of Robert Gordon (see Gordon 2015 for a summary; and Gordon 2016). He argues that this slowdown is independent of economic organization but that its effects will be made worse by six negative headwinds in the United States: an ageing population, a declining role for educational improvement, rising inequality, the shift in production overseas, energy and environmental restrictions, and private and state debt. Gordon treats these headwinds in a very conventional way. He laments the difficulties of the US education system, but educational improvement must follow the now familiar S-shaped curve as we move from mass illiteracy to mass higher education. His concern with energy and environmental regulation also suggests that he still thinks of the economy as a system rather than a subsystem. His arguments about debt seem to reflect a partial "austerity economics". But let us set this aside. Gordon is right to argue that, for an economist, it is his emphasis on the growing limits of technological change that is unorthodox. Gordon suggests that we have passed through the three industrial revolutions set out in Table 4.5.

The biggest gains came from IR2 (the second industrial revolution). Gordon's vision here is much wider than that of many economists. The transformative and liberating power of piped water and piped sewage rarely figure in textbook accounts of productivity growth but they have been central to the improvement of human life. This matters historically. It also matters when we look at productivity problems in poor countries. His bigger point is that these changes often produced gains that cannot be replicated. Before the invention of the steam engine the physical transport of people, goods and information was limited to the carrying and pulling capacity and speed

**Table 4.5** Robert Gordon's three industrial revolutions

|  | Key technologies | Breakthrough era | Widening and deepening era of subsidiary and complementary developments |
|---|---|---|---|
| IR1 | Steam | 1750–1830 | 1830–1930s |
| IR2 | Electricity<br>Petrol engines<br>Water and sewage<br>Petroleum products<br>Communications and entertainment | 1870–1900 | 1900–1970s |
| IR3 | Computers and internet | 1960s–1990s | 1990s to date and beyond |

of the horse. IR1 and IR2 then increased the speed of information transmission from weeks to minutes (the telegraph): a much bigger shift than that created by the internet. They increased the speed of physical movement of people and goods but the limits of this were reached long ago. The speed of air travel, for example, peaked at the turn of the 1960s. We can qualify these big points in numerous ways, but would this detract from Gordon's central point that the big changes have already been made?

IR3, he argues, is of a much more modest size. Digital systems continue to improve but the biggest gains came with the breakthrough applications. Much of the hype associated with the digital economy now relates to its use in leisure and entertainment. Gordon, and some other economists, also argue that recent technological change has been capital saving and had a narrower impact compared to the past. An Amazon warehouse requires less capital and has fewer net spillover effects than the development of big shopping centres.

While economists tend to think that technological change can go on and on, for many scientists the idea of the limits of technical and scientific advance is more orthodox. Once big insights have been applied to technology it becomes harder to do better what is already been done well. In terms of scientific knowledge, "low-hanging fruit" have been plucked so that the future advance of knowledge has to be more incremental. There may also, some think, be limits to our human understanding.

Others see the problem more in terms of how both basic science and applied research and development is organized. Big money is thrown after some kinds of advances while others are neglected. Big money also supports "bad science" and forms of regressive technological change, as with military technologies and the inducements in medicine to overtreat and overmedicalize, for example. Commercial secrecy prevents the sharing of successes but, as important, also leads to a lack a sharing of the knowledge of failures and the ability to learn from them.

The contrasting visions of future advance between economists and many scientists can be seen in the contradiction between Moore's law and Eroom's law. Moore's law is beloved of techo-enthusiast economists. It suggests that the number of transistors on a microchip has doubled every two years. This has been a significant part of the advance in digital technology and a wonderful example of exponential growth. Unfortunately, it is an empirical observation of a short period of advance. That period has already come to an end. Scientists realized more quickly than economists that even when the doubling was occurring something else was happening. Some named this Eroom's law (Moore's law in reverse). Eroom's law suggests that over time to get the same (or an even smaller) advance you have to put a lot more in. The evidence for this lies partly in the research and development spending needed, partly in the size of the research teams needed. Researchers need longer training. The number of patents per researcher is falling. It has been suggested too that the average age of Nobel Prize winners in science has been rising, reflecting the greater difficulties of early career researchers making new breakthroughs and the long periods needed to confirm early insights. Yet, with continued faith in technical progress, most economists are reluctant to recognize that research productivity is falling.

A second approach to the possibility of secular stagnation also emphasizes the supply side. But it sees both slowing overall growth and slowing productivity growth as being caused by the same set of endogenous, organizational factors. According to this view, maturing capitalist economies become subject to increasing rigidity. Schumpeter called it the problem of "arterial sclerosis". He thought the social and political forces created by capitalism would put pressure on the state to modify the initial dynamism of any entrepreneur-led creative destruction. Others, supporters of free enterprise too, have focused on what they see as the restricting role of the state and the pressures towards oligopoly and monopoly. They focus on the negative productivity effects of slow deregulation in sectors like technical services, retail, energy, transport and legal and accountancy services. Yet it is not clear that many would be enthusiastic about a greater free-for-all in any of these sectors. Indeed, given the recent lamentable performance in some of them, they might benefit from greater regulation.

More critical radical accounts disparage the arguments about the "anti-capitalist" thrust of the state, suggesting that too often it is supportive of private power rather than limiting it. But they too have stressed how "monopoly capitalism" undermines the dynamism of technical change and productivity growth (Despain 2015). Whatever the merits (or demerits) of these arguments, there is an obvious problem. These organizational constraints have long been in existence and it is not clear that pressures from them have shifted to a higher level in recent decades.

One version of this focus on organizational limits, however, does address this issue. This is the argument that in the last decades we have seen a structural shift towards a new emphasis on financialization and rent seeking. A wide variety of accounts stress this aspect, although they differ in its explanation. What they share is the view that we have seen a movement from a focus on expanding profits by creating new value to one where the emphasis is on financial gains and the exploitation of strategic position. The growing role of the financial sector itself and its focus on "profits without producing" is part of this story, but the arguments go much wider. In this account the state becomes a vehicle that can be milked to make private gains but socialize losses. Companies look to profit from control of intellectual property. Top managers look to make short-term gains. They are encouraged to manipulate share prices rather than doing new things or old things better. Profits are used for shareholder payouts or held internally (sometimes offshore) and used for "other things", including speculation (Mazzucato 2018a; Stiglitz 2019).

The third approach to the possibility of secular stagnation looks at the demand-side view and endogenous macroeconomic factors. In the nineteenth century, Marx speculated that there might be a tendency for the long-term rate of profit to fall in the system. He recognized that there were countervailing pressures, but some Marxist economists have argued that there is evidence that the long-run rate of profit has been falling over the past decades and this is weakening the dynamism of capitalism. Keynes and post-Keynesian economists also share the view that capitalism will not always deliver high growth. It was Keynes' great insight in the 1930s that capitalism could just as easily deliver low growth, surplus capacity and unemployment. This view was taken up by Alvin Hansen at the time, who combined it with a focus on structural factors like the closing of the American frontier and slower population growth to develop the initial theory of "secular stagnation".

But after the Second World War, fears of "secular stagnation" gave way to a celebration of what Paul Samuelson called "secular exhilaration". Models built around the idea of tendencies towards stagnation tended to be marginalized. They became more so in the 1980s and 1990s when the neoliberal counter-revolution led to a rejection of much Keynesian thinking and a general endorsement of market dynamics, including its productivity dynamics.

The shock of the scale of the 2008 crisis forced a rethink and shifted attention back to these earlier themes. The crisis required extraordinary levels of state intervention to keep the banking system afloat, but instead of recovery being rapid it has been uneven and protracted. Interest rates have been at unprecedentedly low levels and inflation has remained low. There seems to be a pattern of excess savings and low investment, and so the gap between actual output and potential output is rising. In 2012 two leading analysts in the Bank of England in the UK wrote that "the economics profession has for much of the twentieth century been bewitched by normality. Over the past five years, the real world has behaved in ways that made a monkey of these theories" (Haldane & Nelson 2012: 14). A mainstream interest in "secular stagnation" ideas seemed to be validated the next year when one of the world's leading economists, Larry Summers, wrote a series of popular articles about it. He not only referred back to Hansen but echoed his fears that "the essence of secular stagnation [is] sick recoveries which die in their infancy". For Summers this tendency to secular stagnation does not reflect an "inherent flaw", it is "not a fate to which we ought to be resigned". Joseph Stiglitz has called it "stagnation by design" (Stiglitz 2014).

Austerity policies have perpetuated and intensified the underlying problems. In the household sector, growing income inequality allows the richest to value different forms of savings over investment. In the private sector we find zombie firms that should have gone to the wall but which have been kept alive by low interest rates. Where private companies are more dynamic, they still underinvest, sitting on cash hoards or using their financial resources in different forms of speculation. State expenditure is cut back so that there is limited investment, if any, in infrastructure. Housing markets remain distorted and the reluctance to spend on social welfare contributes towards problems in the quality and quantity of the labour supply.

Governments have not been using the power they have to correct this. Summers is very much an establishment figure so his solutions involve modest policy corrections to what he sees as policy mistakes. Others, like Joseph Stiglitz, look to still deeper reforms, albeit within the system. The question is whether either is enough.

## Joining the two arguments?

This has been a chapter of two halves. In the first half we looked at the argument that the planet cannot support infinite productivity growth. In the second half we looked at the argument that productivity growth is already slowing at the frontier for the most advanced economies. Economists are very bad at joining these two arguments together. They are trapped by the alienated view we noted in Chapter 1 and the confusion of ends and means. Robert Gordon, for example, projects a "pessimistic" scenario forwards in which weakening productivity growth leads to an output per head for the US in 2100 of $87,000. He describes this as "frightening" because it implies only a doubling of output per head over the rest of the century compared to the faster growth in the previous one. What is more frightening is his failure to see the implications of what he is saying. Is it possible to double US output per head within the limits of the planet? And could this ever be generalized to the planet as a whole? To his credit Gordon does recognize that the recent disproportionate capture of productivity gains by those at the top is a problem, but this only points to the need to ask why we are making such poor use of the productivity potential we already have. The same confusion is evident when economists suggest that we need to restore a lost productivity vigour through more deregulation and labour and product market flexibility. Regulation seems for them to be a perverse plot to hold back productivity rather than an attempt, however halting, to direct it to better ends.

An alternative view is to see the pressures on productivity growth not as a problem but as an invitation to do something different and to do so with all the more urgency given the problems set out at the start of this chapter. One way of thinking about this is in terms of a "green new deal". In Chapter 8 we will ask whether such a new deal is enough, but here let us briefly look at the positive case for it. The argument for a green new deal is that we do not have to wait to shift priorities. What is needed now is a massive programme of investment in renewable energies, public infrastructure and improved housing, and the protection of the global commons. This could sustain economic activity without having the same negative effects on the environment. It would also be more productive if we widen our vision about what real productivity improvement actually entails.

Many of the technologies to make a difference already exist and some are in use in some parts of the world. The problem is to take them up on a sufficient scale globally. In 2011, the Institute of Mechanical Engineers in the UK said:

> even though the Institute of Mechanical Engineers believes that there are no insurmountable technical issues in sourcing enough

energy for an increasingly affluent larger global population, and providing it to where it is needed, the solutions that will deliver a successful outcome are by no means simple. The difficulties lie in the areas of regulation, financing, politics, social ethics and inter-national relations.                                        (Quoted in Dorling 2013: 220)

The logic of this argument is that we need to join together our thinking about productivity and its limits and possibilities. This, however, requires a new political vision. It requires economists and policy-makers to break with the narrowness of their existing views. There is some evidence that some are doing this, but the power of old ways of thinking remains strong. They are underpinned by powerful interests. We live in a world where the issue of productivity is tied up not only with capitalism as an "economic" system but also with interstate competition, where the issue of "the productivity of nations" seems central. It is to this that we now turn in Chapters 5–7, starting with the question of productivity and its role in the most advanced national economies.

# 5

# It's tough at the top

We have seen that there are significant gaps in the productivity levels between economies. These gaps developed qualitatively, and then quantitatively, as capitalism took off and more and more of the world was dragged into its orbit. This produced the "great divergence" or "divergence big time". The gap between the most productive and least productive economies in the world economy has continued to grow.

Between the extremes, states compete to catch up or minimize the threat of falling back. The economies that have closed the gap are sometimes grouped into "convergence clubs". Talk of "clubs" implies that there is some commonality, some membership criteria, but critics quickly pointed out that economies were being grouped together once they had grown or failed to grow. They were clubs "after the event" not "before it".

The catching-up process of productivity growth certainly involves some common elements. But it has taken place, and is taking place, in a dynamic global economy so the possibilities and constraints have also varied over time and place. Moses Abramovitz argued that an economy not only needs the capability to catch up, it needs the opportunity (Abramovitz 1986). In this chapter we will focus on economies at the top of the global productivity hierarchy, their past productivity growth and some aspects of the current debates about their productivity performance.

## Britain and the United States: the leaders of the gang?

In the last two centuries two economies have dominated any global productivity race: Britain and the United States. Britain's dominance lasted until the late nineteenth century, but since then the US has set, and continues to set, the global productivity benchmarks.

Britain's early productivity lead was bound up with it being "the first industrial nation". However, the underlying productivity story is rather different from that often suggested. Table 5.1 shows some very long-run data for the British economy. These estimates look more precise than they really are, but we can use them to make some important points about the emergence of Britain's early productivity lead.

**Table 5.1** Sectoral shares and labour productivity growth in Britain, 1381–1851

|      | Labour force shares | | | Output shares | | | Labour productivity growth | | |
|------|------|--------|-------|------|--------|-------|------|--------|-------|
|      | Ag.  | Indus. | Serv. | Ag.  | Indus. | Serv. | Ag.  | Indus. | Serv. |
| 1381 | 57.2 | 19.2   | 23.6  | 45.5 | 28.8   | 25.7  | 1381–1700 | | |
| 1522 | 58.1 | 22.7   | 19.2  | 39.7 | 38.7   | 21.6  | 0.09 | 0.10 | 0.16 |
| 1700 | 38.9 | 34.0   | 27.2  | 26.7 | 41.3   | 32.0  |      |      |      |
| 1759 | 36.8 | 33.9   | 29.3  | 29.7 | 35.2   | 35.1  | 1700–1851 | | |
| 1801 | 31.7 | 36.4   | 31.9  | 31.4 | 32.7   | 36.0  | 0.55 | 0.87 | 0.62 |
| 1851 | 23.5 | 45.6   | 30.9  | 18.7 | 32.1   | 49.2  |      |      |      |

Source: Broadberry et al. (2013).

Note first the contrast between the rate of productivity growth before 1700 and that which came after, which is further evidence of the productivity shift that occurred with industrialization. Notice too that labour productivity growth after 1700 picked up in all sectors. We can see that it was productivity growth in industry that was fastest (the "industrial revolution"), but the pick-up of productivity growth in agriculture and services (the "agricultural" and a possible "service" revolution) was important too. The third point is that the rate of increase between 1700 and 1851 – although substantial compared to the past – looks less impressive when compared to later cases. The intra-sector rate of change was often patchier than we imagine: IR1 affected the smaller part of industrial production in Britain before 1851. The fourth point is that the structure of the British economy was already precociously modern compared to its contemporaries. The low labour force and output shares in agriculture were quite unusual. This was also reflected in the advanced level of urbanization in Britain: it became the world's first urban economy in 1851. This leads to a fifth important point in terms of the gap between Britain and its near competitors. The composition effect and the greater share of labour in low-productivity peasant agriculture in Europe meant that the productivity gap for the British economy as a whole looks rather greater than if the gaps in industry and services are compared. Britain's early lead was partly because it appeared to be "the workshop of the world" but also because it had a relatively advanced and smaller rural sector. Compared with the great divergences in the rest of the world that were developing, those between the British economy and its nearest competitors were relatively modest.

If we accept the conventional productivity measurements, Britain retained its role as European productivity leader until after the Second World War. Globally, from the 1890s, it took second place to the US. Ignoring the trend changes we referred to in Chapter 4, the long-run annual rate of labour productivity growth for the US economy between 1860 and 2007 was around 1.9 per cent. The share of global GDP produced in the United States rose from 2 per cent in 1820 to 19 per cent in 1913 and some 27 per cent in 1950. Table 5.2 shows labour productivity per worker for the economy as a whole and for selected sectors for Britain and Germany as a percentage of the US level. We can see that the size of the UK lead over Germany varies, but it was overtaken by the US in the late nineteenth century. The table also brings out the composition effect.

The analysis from which Table 5.2 is drawn also has data for six other sectors. Those selected for our table show that the US has also been characterized

**Table 5.2** Labour productivity per worker in UK and Germany as a percentage of the US level, for economy as a whole and selected sectors, 1871–1990

|      | GDP | | Agricultural sector | | Manufacturing sector | | Finance/services sector | |
| --- | --- | --- | --- | --- | --- | --- | --- | --- |
|      | UK | Germany | UK | Germany | UK | Germany | UK | Germany |
| 1871 | 111 | 66 | 115 | 64 | 55 | 51 | 156 | na |
| 1890 | 93 | 56 | 98 | 53 | 52 | 49 | 188 | 87 |
| 1910 | 85 | 64 | 97 | 65 | 49 | 58 | 128 | 67 |
| 1937 | 75 | 57 | 97 | 55 | 48 | 49 | 104 | 56 |
| 1950 | 60 | 45 | 79 | 32 | 38 | 36 | 90 | 47 |
| 1973 | 66 | 75 | 76 | 38 | 47 | 56 | 85 | 75 |
| 1990 | 75 | 94 | 66 | 50 | 57 | 62 | 99 | 110 |

*Source*: Author's recalculations from Broadberry (1998) for which see for detailed and additional data.

by high labour productivity in agriculture and that it belatedly developed a lead in services and finance too. The table may overstate the lead because it is a calculation per worker and not hours, an important issue to which we will return, but it seems clear that the peak gap between the US and its immediate challengers came in the 1950s.

This was when Stephen Sondheim and Leonard Bernstein had the Puerto Rican migrants sing about the merits (and some of the demerits) of the US lead in the musical *West Side Story*:

> Skyscrapers bloom in America
> Cadillacs zoom in America
> Industry boom in America
> Twelve in a room in America.

But this was also the peak of the Cold War when it seemed that the US might be challenged by the rapid catch-up of the USSR. Nevertheless, there was a confidence that if productivity growth continued there was little that could not be done. "We choose to go to the moon in this decade and do other things not because they are easy, but because they are hard", said President Kennedy expressing the self-confidence of the time in 1962.

"What made the United States unique was the combination of resource abundance and large markets", said Paul Romer (1996: 8). The first and most obvious factor here is size. Since the completion of the formation of the United States, by conquest and purchase, it has been the world's fourth largest country in terms of area. Its combination of climate, ease of communication and natural resources means that it is one of, if not the, best endowed of all. A second size dimension is population. By both natural increase and migration (despite the fate of the indigenous population) the US became the fourth largest country in the world in terms of population in the 1860s. It remained in this position until 1991 when the collapse of the USSR made it the third largest. On the demand side too, the domestic market has tended to a greater degree of homogeneity as well as size.

But already by the mid-nineteenth century the US was in the lead in terms of manufacturing productivity. The conventional explanation for this, often called the Habakkuk thesis after the economic historian who first set it out more fully, is that the availability of free land meant that US employers had to offer higher wages and compensate for this by labour-saving technologies that led to higher levels of labour productivity (Habakkuk 1962). Early on the US became path dependent on a higher level of capital intensity per worker. It is easy then to see why the US economy led the way with standardization and interchangeable parts, and forms of mass production. It also helps us to understand why the US has pioneered forms of business organization. The fact that the US has been and remains such a powerhouse has also led to it being a magnet in the global economy. If leadership imposes a burden it also brings with it many advantages. Consider one: migration. In 2005, the US House of Representatives even thanked the contribution of Indians, and Indian IT graduates in particular, who had come to America for their role in "economic innovation" and "helping to advance and enrich American society".

What should we add beyond this? Many commentators have emphasized more intangible mystery ingredients: the positive nature of American institutions, culture, markets, entrepreneurial zeal and so on. Such factors are hard to define. They are even harder to measure and to decide what is cause and what is effect? Even if such factors can be shown to be both sufficiently different and positive it is hard to know how big a role they have played and continued to play. This type of analysis too often feeds into dubious notions of American exceptionalism. We should also not forget the argument that, belying free market claims, the US has a "hidden development state" (Block 2008). US industry was protected until after the Second World War. The state also undertook other forms of support and in more recent times the military-industrial complex has piled resources into technological advance.

## The long boom and the convergence of European productivity levels

Table 5.2 also shows that after 1950 the productivity gaps between the US and the UK and Germany closed, although more impressively for Germany than the UK. This was both an economy-wide closing and a sectoral one. It was part of a general catching-up process for a bigger group of European economies as well as Japan and the USSR, which we will come to separately. The period from 1945 to the early 1970s was a unique one in economic history. At the time the successes were spoken of as "economic miracles". In France these years are described as the *Trente Glorieuses*. In Germany they are called the *Wirtschaftswunder*. By the 1970s the productivity gaps between the most successful advanced economies had closed to similar levels that exist today.

A vicious circle of comparative failure in the 1930s seemed to have given way to a virtuous circle of success after 1945. The mystery of why deepened in the next decades, when the productivity surges faltered and the overall performance of the world economy became more uneven. Today we can see more clearly what was involved within the virtuous circle even if the debates as to what caused the shifts into it and out of it are still ongoing (Crafts & Toniolo 1996; Temin 2002).

In the boom years, GDP growth was strong. The global economy was more buoyant and stable than it had been before or has been since. Initially Marshall Aid helped recovery in western Europe. World trade had fallen in the 1930s. Now it grew at 8 per cent per year. There was a deepening of global ties and a shift in the centre of gravity away from colonial connections to an intensification of linkages between the most advanced economies. The advanced productivity frontier seemed to expand steadily. In 1957 the European Economic Community was formed as a partial step to deeper regional integration. Eliminating internal tariffs and creating a common external tariff can lead to what economists call trade diversion. More efficient producers outside the union lose out to less efficient ones inside the union as production is reallocated because of the effect of the external tariff. This is a loss to global welfare and a reduction in global productivity because of an increasing misallocation of resources. If integration results in inefficient producers within the union being squeezed out by more efficient internal producers, then this is trade creation: it increases global welfare and it increases overall productivity through specialization. This is what seems to have happened with the development of the European Union, despite the continuing protective nature of some of its elements, not least the common agricultural policy. But (as with our earlier discussion of static and dynamic efficiency) the bigger gains probably come from dynamic efficiency improvements. A larger market with fewer barriers, greater competition, the development of extended production chains, cooperative research and development and, later, labour mobility have all helped to push productivity up among member states and to emulate some of the elements of the huge US market.

After 1945, the European economies were able to sustain high rates of investment in the economic infrastructure – from transport to housing

– aimed at recovering from the war and overcoming the legacy of the more distant past. High rates of investment also enabled states and businesses to embody new technologies and new organizational forms, whether in agriculture, manufacturing or parts of service activity. This involved a certain amount of copying through the "Americanization" process. But because these were already relatively advanced economies some of the changes also drew on internally generated innovations. Allen points out, for example, that in the car industry – often seen as the embodiment of change in the decades either side of the Second World War – significant advances were also made in France, Germany and Britain and some other countries as well as the US (Allen 2011). This was complemented by ongoing social improvements in health, education and welfare, all of which too seem to have had positive productivity effects. These changes were given added punch by the ability of the European economies (other than the UK) to shift resources out of lower-productivity agriculture. "In the large continental countries, agriculture and self-employment furnished a great reservoir of workers that could be tapped to provide the labour supply needed to swell non-farm production with little loss of output in the activities from which this labour was drawn" (Denison 1968: 256). It was the western European economies that caught up the most. The economies in southern Europe still have some way to go. Productivity levels in Greece, Portugal and Turkey are even more behind, although all of these economies are, in global terms, now part of the rich world club.

But for the most successful European economies the bigger effects of catch-up have now been exhausted. It was perfectly natural for growth rates in these advanced economies to slow down as they converged on the productivity frontier. This removes a lot of the mystery in the debates about individual national "success" and "failure". It still leaves unresolved the question of why a less benign overall climate has developed since the 1970s and the speed at which the most advanced economies now move.

## Japanese success

The Western bloc was held together by the polarization against the Soviet bloc. Yet productivity catch-up still created some tensions. West Germany had been on the losing side in 1945, now it seemed to be winning. However, one country above all others stands out for the dynamism of its overall productivity catch-up. In economic terms Japan was "the greatest success of the twentieth century" (Allen 2011: 6). For the US to be challenged by "the emerging Japanese super state" seemed all the more galling to some in the US given the dismissive views of Japan in American culture and memory, but "Japan" was still viewed positively as part of the "West".

Japan was the only economy which, starting its industrialization in the late nineteenth century, managed to more or less close the gap with the advanced economies. So spectacular was its success that at one point it seemed that Americanization might give way to "Japanization" as a model for productivity growth emulation. Figure 5.1 shows the catch-up in GDP per head levels for Japan as well as the USSR/Russia.

From the 1850s, Japan came under Western economic, political and military pressure. For a pre-industrial society, it had already achieved a significant level of development under the Tokogawa regime (1603–1868). The level of urbanization was around 15 per cent, literacy ran at 50 per cent and there was a sophisticated economic and social system. The result was that Japan was not colonized like India, nor was it pulled apart like China. Instead the shock of the threat of Western penetration led to a revolution from above in 1868 which laid the basis for reforms. In most of the Meiji period (1868–1905), Western interests had sufficient power to stop the Japanese state from using tariffs to build up their economy. But they were able to import, copy and adapt Western technologies on a considerable

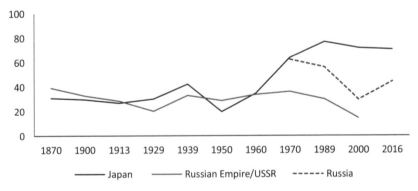

**Figure 5.1** Japanese and USSR/Russia GDP per head as percentage of US level, 1870–2016
*Source*: Maddison database updated.

scale. Then in the "imperial period" (1905–45) Japan's rulers were better able to realize their dream of "a strong army-strong economy". The share of manufacturing in total output rose from 20 per cent in 1914 to 35 per cent in 1938. In the weak global economy Japan's growth was sufficient to enable it to challenge the US in the Second World War. That it did so reflected the social and political contradictions of the time which led to an aggressive imperialist drive with its rulers desiring to be a great power whatever the costs. The results in the Second World War are well known.

Defeated and prostrate in 1945, Japan quickly recovered as part of the Western alliance in the Cold War years. Between 1950 and 1990 the economy grew at an average 5.9 per cent a year. Growth was fastest between 1953 and 1973 when it was 8 per cent per year. This occurred because of an intensification of elements present earlier. There was a huge push in terms of capital investment. There was also a huge increase in the quantity and quality of the labour input. There was large-scale technological borrowing too. Without this, Japan could not have grown. Technology was modified and adapted and combined with home-grown improvements such as just-in-time delivery methods.

This drive was not planned in the same way as Soviet industrialization was but there was a significant degree of central direction, although its extent declined over time. The Japanese Ministry of Trade and Industry, working with large Japanese corporate groups, encouraged a broad pattern of development and the achieving of significant economies of scale through the development of large modern plants.

Why was this so successful? There were several reasons. As Abramovitz said, opportunities and capacities are always important. The opportunities arose because after Japan's defeat in 1945 it was not allowed to spend a huge amount on its military but rather lived under US military protection. This enabled it to develop a heavy industrial and consumer-based economy based on a virtuous circle of high productivity–high wages. It enjoyed significant US aid in the 1950s as well as benefiting from US military spending in Japan. US protection also extended to a sympathetic view of Japanese exports even as they began to compete with US home production. By 1970, for example, a third of Japanese steel production was being exported. This meant that Japan was able to encourage a more outward-looking pattern of development that could take advantage of the shifts in the global economy that became evident in the late twentieth century.

But the logic of our analysis is that slowdown was inevitable as the gains from the mobilization and transfer of resources were exhausted and the technological gaps closed. In the event, financial crisis and the collapse of a bubble economy in 1991–2 prefigured elements of the global crisis of 2008. Since then high growth rates have not resumed. But the performance of the economy has in comparative terms still been positive. A productivity gap still remains, but some commentators admire the way that Japan has negotiated the transition to slower rates of growth and less spectacular productivity improvements.

## Back in the USSR: the price of failure

In the Cold War it was the challenge of the USSR which caused the greatest concerns. In the event the USSR, and the Soviet bloc formed after 1945, eventually collapsed. Its chequered career is set out in Figure 5.1, alongside that of Japan. The ups and downs of the USSR/Russia are clear. Yet the manner in which the Soviet bloc closed the gap for a time remains important historically. It is also interesting because, despite the collapse of the Soviet bloc in 1989–91, its productivity story prefigured elements we have seen in Japan and which we will see even more when we turn to the more recent Asian success stories. The key difference was that the Soviet bloc was forced to compete in much more hostile circumstances.

If in 1917 the Russian Revolution seemed to offer the prospect of a different world, from 1928–9 onwards the Soviet leadership tried to drive the economy forwards through central direction. They perceived themselves to be under the constant threat of war, first from Nazi Germany and then from the US and NATO. They had to work in relative isolation partly because of these political conflicts but also due to external economic difficulties (Haynes 2017). Productivity growth was seen as central to any success. In 1935, Stalin said, "Why can and should and necessarily will socialism conquer the capitalist system of economy? Because it can give ... a higher productivity of labour." Let us leave aside the question of whether Stalin's Russia represented any form of socialism. There is still an essential insight here that competitive survival externally, and popular acquiescence if not support internally, depended on modernizing the economy and creating a high-productivity society.

The achievements in the 1930s enabled the USSR to play the key role in the defeat of Nazi Germany. After the war, growth in the USSR and the Soviet bloc continued to surge forwards. At the point when the contrast between the growth rates with the US was especially sharp – in the late 1950s – the head of the CIA warned that, "if the Soviet industrial growth rate persists at eight or nine percent per annum over the next decade ... the gap between our two economies ... will be dangerously narrowed" (quoted in Krugman 1994b: 65). In the event, from the 1970s growth in the USSR (and across the Soviet bloc) slowed, and at the end of the 1980s the bloc went into a crisis and eventual collapse.

Tracking the rise and fall of the economy of the Soviet bloc poses formidable measurement problems. There were some statistical sleights of hand, different concepts were used and the state-controlled nature of these economies meant that prices were distorted. Problems arose too because of the difficulty of measuring economic progress and productivity growth when the structure of the economy was changing very fast. Trying to solve these problems led economists to think through aspects of productivity analysis in ways that have become incorporated into our wider understanding of economic change.

Nevertheless, from 1928 to the 1970s, with the exception of Japan, Soviet bloc economic successes were greater than anywhere else at this time. Static inefficiencies there might have been, but there also seemed to be dynamic efficiencies (Allen 2003). With hindsight, Soviet bloc performance looks no better than the Asian economies that grew later. But this does not mean that the same opportunities existed then. The potential for catch-up productivity is dependent on time and place. In the 1930s the USSR's success, although exaggerated, was real. And after 1945, at least until the 1970s, its performance and that of its satellites was not only better than in the past but better than Latin America, Africa and most of Asia.

Today we can see more clearly that the most important elements involved in Soviet-type growth were less peculiar than was claimed at the time. The first was massively increased investment in infrastructure, new factories and military machinery, and the mechanization of agriculture (if partly to replace the animals killed by the peasants in their resistance to collectivization). The second was a massive increase in the labour input by mobilizing previously underutilized rural and urban labour and female labour with migration to the towns and the new factories. Third, there was a huge effort to increase labour force quality through raising educational standards, both at the basic level of mass literacy but then increased schooling and further and higher education. Labour force quality was also affected by socialization into new forms of work discipline and modern life. The service sector was deliberately held back so that the switch was more from agriculture to industry, giving a significant productivity boost. All this involved significant human cost. Mass repression was at its greatest in the USSR in 1936–53, but elements of repression appeared in other bloc states. All of this was then combined with deliberate technological emulation and copying, whether based on buying in whole plants, borrowing ideas openly or getting them by espionage. At the time much was made of Soviet technological inferiority, but this was quite natural in a catch-up society. What is perhaps more remarkable is the sustained effort devoted to research and development and its successes, even if it was concentrated in the military-industrial sector.

Why then did it fail? The negative effects of the Cold War and the pressures to compete militarily and economically in conditions of relative isolation are important. In 1991 too many believed the answer was "systemic failure" and that privatization and markets would unleash a new dynamism, but Figure 5.1 shows that this did not happen. Some now argue that there were fatal policy mistakes. In 1960 the exiled Russian economist Wassily Leontief said the Soviet economy is "directed with ruthless and determined skill". But later bad economic policy choices have been argued to have contributed to the political crisis that brought down the USSR (Allen 2003). Whatever the explanation, the challenge today to the power of the "West" comes from even further "East": from Beijing.

## Comparative productivity at the top today

In the competition between rich world economies today, much of the obsession with small differences in the absolute level of productivity seems misplaced. Table 5.3 shows that if we look at output per worker then big differences between GDP per capita in the rich world still seem to exist. But when we look at output per hour worked then the gaps suddenly reduce and may even disappear.

Table 5.4 shows that the hours inputs have fallen everywhere, but there remains a quite extraordinary variation in the number of hours worked in

**Table 5.3** Members of the rich world club: possible measures of productivity as percentage of US level for 2017

|  | GDP per capita | GDP per person employed | GDP per hour worked |
|---|---|---|---|
| Norway | 121 | 108 | 134 |
| US | 100 | 100 | 100 |
| Netherlands | 89 | 80 | 98 |
| Germany | 83 | 75 | 97 |
| Sweden | 87 | 84 | 91 |
| Belgium | 78 | 90 | 102 |
| UK | 73 | 72 | 76 |
| France | 71 | 81 | 95 |
| Japan | 72 | 65 | 65 |

*Source*: US Conference Board

rich countries. We can see in particular that "New World" countries have a culture of working more hours, especially in the United States. Once account is taken of this, the level of US productivity no longer seems so superior.

In fact, the picture may be even better. The hours input in rich economies is measured through self-reporting in the Labour Force Survey. It appears that issues like adjusting for holidays, sick leave, strikes and work in the "grey-black" economy are not always done in the same way. Both the UK and Sweden may have overstated their hours input compared to that in other countries where bigger adjustments have been made. If this argument is correct then the productivity gaps for the UK might be reduced by a half, say, with France.

**Table 5.4** Annual hours of work, 1870–2000, selected countries

|  | Europe | | | | | "New World" | | |
|---|---|---|---|---|---|---|---|---|
|  | UK | France | Germany | Netherlands | Italy | US | Canada | Australia |
| 1870 | 2,755 | 3,168 | 3,284 | 3,274 | 3,000 | 3,096 | 2,845 | 2,792 |
| 1913 | 2,656 | 2,933 | 2,723 | 2,942 | 2,953 | 2,900 | 2,868 | 2,214 |
| 1938 | 2,200 | 1,760 | 2,187 | 2,281 | 2,162 | 1,756 | 2,212 | 2,109 |
| 1950 | 2,112 | 2,045 | 2,372 | 2,156 | 1,951 | 2,008 | 2,111 | 2,023 |
| 1973 | 1,919 | 1,849 | 1,808 | 1,709 | 1,825 | 1,942 | 1,874 | 1,837 |
| 2000 | 1,653 | 1,443 | 1,463 | 1,352 | 1,612 | 1,878 | 1,825 | 1,797 |

*Source*: Huberman and Minns (2005, 2007).

In Chapter 4 we suggested that in recent decades there has also been a convergence in productivity growth rates between rich economies. Table 5.5 shows the most recent data. Clearly there are gaps, but they are nothing like they were in the past.

**Table 5.5** Members of the rich world club: annual percentage change in GDP per hour worked, 2000–17

|  | All mature economies | US | Japan | EU-28 | Euro area | UK | Germany | France |
|---|---|---|---|---|---|---|---|---|
| 2000–7 | 2.2 | 2.5 | 2.1 | 1.8 | 1.4 | 2.1 | 1.7 | 1.5 |
| 2008–15 | 1.1 | 1.3 | 1.3 | 0.7 | 0.6 | 0.1 | 0.6 | 0.5 |
| 2016 | 0.9 | 0.3 | 0.6 | 1.2 | 1.0 | 0.6 | 1.2 | 1.0 |
| 2017 | 1.1 | 1.0 | 0.9 | 1.3 | 0.2 | 0.6 | 1.4 | 0.2 |

*Source*: US Conference Board.

Why might the gaps at the top now be so small? Despite the apparent quirks that make countries interesting to visit, what stands out in economic terms is their similarity by level. In any rich world club, economic structures are similar, as are levels of urbanization. The quantity and quality of inputs are broadly comparable. Think of the nature of the labour force, level of education, health, etc. So too is the quantity and quality of output. Rich club economies are more closely integrated into the global economy. In agriculture, manufacturing and parts of the service industries like banking and business services, multinationals dominate activity. Where plants and offices are linked there is considerable pressure to achieve the same levels of productivity when doing comparable things. Exchange rate variations, labour costs and poorer social security benefits can compensate to some extent for productivity variation, but they will not overcome intra-company productivity gaps on a long-term basis. The pressure instead is to eliminate intra-company gaps by raising "the local game".

## The British productivity failure?

There is, however, one advanced country that seems to stand out rather more in terms of weak performance: Britain. Productivity has continued to advance, subject to ups and downs, but its relatively weak position today is evident in Table 5.4. It is said that Britain's productivity level is such that it takes five days in the UK to do what is done in four in France. If we take account of the possible mismeasurement, we might reduce the gap to 4.5 days, but this is still a considerable difference.

It is important here to consider two different ways of thinking about any "British problem". The first is the changing structure of the economy. Britain's early industrialization meant that it developed a huge manufacturing sector. The share of labour in industry peaked in 1955 at 48 per cent. The subsequent loss of manufacturing employment had a social affect as regions based on traditional industries went into decline. It had huge psychological affect too, although today the manufacturing share, despite being much lower than that of Germany, is not out of line with some other advanced economies. The second way of thinking about any UK problem is in terms of productivity. The two are not entirely separate. We know that industry is often the driver of productivity change. UK governments have, for decades, been happy to reflect the interests of the City of London even if they have weakened "manufacturing" capital through, for example, the overvaluation of the pound. But it is the overall productivity problem that is our concern here.

A significant part of the discussion of the UK economy in the long boom years was dominated by a growing concern with productivity. With hindsight many economic historians think this misplaced. Those who argued at the time that a small economy which had industrialized first could not expect to stay in the lead forever seem to have better grasped that a degree of relative decline was inevitable. Moreover, looked at in comparative terms the productivity performance – at least until late on in the boom – does not seem to have been that bad. Still, the perception that there was a "British disease", defined quite differently by Left and Right, grew in force. When a new Tory government came to power in 1979, led by Margaret Thatcher, it was able to impose its vision of the need to unleash a new market and entrepreneurial dynamism which would drive the economy forwards. Later these ideas would come to be labelled "neoliberalism". There is always a gap between ideas and real policy, but these ideas found deep roots in Britain. Since then, what is striking is the continuity in UK policy and approach, whatever government has been in power. The result is that today, if we compare the UK to other advanced economies, it more often than not appears to be a European outlier, closer in some respects to the US.

The share of state expenditure in GDP is at the lower end for an advanced European economy. Britain pioneered mass privatization. A formal industrial policy has been eschewed. Markets are more deregulated than most, especially the labour market. Welfare benefit levels are comparatively low, cut back to incentivise people to work. Trade union membership peaked at 12.2 million in 1980 but by 2018 had fallen to nearly half that number. Trade union density is now less than 25 per cent and running at only 13–14 per cent in the private sector. The share of workers covered by collective bargaining fell more in the UK than any other OECD country. The economy has been opened up to foreign capital, some more dubious than others. Part of the "middle class" operates, in Evan Davis's words, as "butlers to a global elite" (Davis 2011). Levels of wealth and income inequality have risen, yet the relative productivity slide has continued. It might look as if the cure has been worse than the disease.

What stands out today is the relative unevenness of the UK. London, where a significant part of state infrastructure spending is also concentrated, is an economic powerhouse. The UK regions struggle behind it. There is unevenness too in industry performance. There is also an irony in the fact that the two industries where the UK has retained some lead – defence and pharmaceuticals – are both those which have benefited from the more limited "entrepreneurial state" that has continued in Britain. Stephen Broadberry, on the other hand, has argued that "Britain's loss of overall productivity leadership … owes more to developments in services than industry" (Broadberry 2006: 15). This even applies to finance and business services. "The UK's poor productivity performance is not confined to manufacturing. Indeed, the UK underperforms in precisely those areas that are generally considered to be its strengths … the UK's productivity … in financial services was ranked 23rd out of 29 countries by the ONS [Office for National Statistics]" (GFC 2017: 6). Some of the practices in these sectors also raise questions about the nature of real productivity. The big four UK accountancy firms have become global leaders in their field but have been implicated in a mass of scandals about conflicting interests and poor standards. We are used to thinking that the centre of the 2008 global financial crisis was the US, but many suspect that key operations went through London.

In 2018, the Bank of England economist, Andy Haldane, described the UK economy as a "hub with no spokes" (Haldane 2018). World-class firms and plants and companies sit alongside poorly performing ones with, compared to other countries, not a great deal in the middle. The belief that the market knows best has led to the view that only world-class businesses really matter. But just as no sports team can be successful if it only puts a couple of world-class players on the field, so the same applies to economies. They too need strength in breadth and depth, and all the more so if a (multinational) star player gets injured, or decides to retire, or moves elsewhere.

At the bottom end the UK economy has produced jobs. The problem is their quality. In the 2010s, a rash of hand car washes began to appear in British cities. Capital-intensive mechanical car washes seemed objectively to perform better: they are environmentally superior and often cheaper than a hand car wash. Hand car washes often exist on the margins of legality, sometimes popping up on waste ground, with their underemployed workers not always paid properly. For some the growth of the hand car wash is a metaphor for the UK economy. Is it, or part of it, trapped in a low-skill–low-productivity–low-wage equilibrium?

On the edge of the formal sector are dog walkers, gardeners, odd-job people and second-hand clothes collectors. In the formal sector too, there has been a huge expansion of low-paid work. Even if they are paid the minimum wage, many such jobs are effectively subsidized by the state through various forms of tax credits. Instead of supporting high-productivity initiatives, the UK state seems to be supporting low-productivity ones. The result is that many people are now trapped in "in-work poverty".

The response to the 2008 economic crisis intensified the UK's productivity problems. Despite the massive bank bailouts, the UK government quickly turned (now against the advice of perhaps a majority of economists) to policies of austerity focused on cutting the government budget deficit. These policies helped to hold down living standards and prevented structural problems being addressed. Remember too that productivity growth seems to be pro-cyclical. Keeping pressure on demand leads to undercapacity and lower productivity. Britain's productivity slowdown is now especially prolonged and sharp compared to other advanced countries (Haldane 2018).

The debate on poor UK productivity has been dominated by a focus on alleged market, organizational and cultural deficiencies. When policies based on these ideas failed to halt the comparative slide, the official responses seemed to reflect the approach of Victorian doctors. The view was that if bleeding the patient did not work, this only showed the need for more bleeding. This partly reflects the dominance of free market ideas.

It also reflects the fact that much productivity analysis focuses on static allocative issues. One alternative is to look more to the macroeconomic environment and not least the persistently low rate of capital formation in the UK. Between 1997 and 2017, for example, gross capital formation in the UK averaged 16.7 per cent of GDP compared to 20.5 per cent in Germany and 21.7 per cent in France. If productivity growth is not embodied in new capital this may not matter; if it *is* embodied in infrastructure, buildings and equipment, then it matters a lot.

## The problem of unevenness in national productivity levels

The comparative unevenness of the UK economy looks unusual. But in all economies, there is unevenness between firms and, since locations differ, between regions. "Bakeries are just as different from each other as bakeries as a whole are different from steel plants", said Zvi Griliches (quoted in Krueger & Taylor 2000: 185). One widely cited study of the US focusing on intra-industry variation, and using data from the 1970s, found that the average ratio of value added per employee or employee hour was 2:1 for the 75th and 25th percentile of plants. It was over 4:1 for the 90:10 percentile and 7:1 for the 95:5 ratio (Syverson 2004).

Some have suggested that unevenness is growing. A recent study of data drawn from 24 countries suggests that in the years 2001–13 productivity in the top 5 per cent of firms in market services grew at 3.6 per cent per annum, and for those in manufacturing at 2.8 per cent per annum. These are impressive rates. But for the other 95 per cent, the rest, "the laggards", the productivity performance was a more anaemic 0.5 per cent in both sectors. "A small cadre of frontier firms are experiencing robust growth but there is an increasing gap between the global frontier and laggard firms" (Andrews *et al.* 2016: 4). In 2017 in the UK one-third of firms had experienced no meaningful productivity growth since 2000 (Haldane 2017: 13). This reflects a phenomenon evident elsewhere: zombie firms that seemingly should have gone under but which are kept alive by low interest rates and market niches. The problem is that if they are allowed to go under will they be replaced with something more productive?

Some explanations of unevenness focus on demand. Weak firms and plants might survive because consumers have a misplaced loyalty to buying inferior products at higher prices. Goods might not be substitutable, and even things like steel and concrete are far from homogenous products. There may also be strong local market imperfections (Syverson 2004). Others look to the supply side to explain unevenness. Local performance can be affected by levels of investment, research and development and managerial competences, etc.

The focus on the representative firm in competitive equilibrium distracts economists from getting to grips with this problem. "One thing I have realised as I have worked with businesses is that they are far from the idealised profit-maximizing automatons of economic theory. Confusion is endemic to firms", says Steven Levitt, one of the most prominent "market" economists in the US (Levitt & Dubner 2015: 77). Business gurus have created fashions and lucrative, and occasionally stellar, consultative careers by claiming to be able to unravel this confusion and to distil the secrets of business excellence. Cynics note that companies identified as at the pinnacle of good practice in one period have a tendency to do less well and on occasion even disappear in the next.

But some patterns are evident. We can see virtuous circles where higher revenues and higher profits combine with greater capital intensity, levels of research and development and managerial competences. The firms and plants at the top are bigger and better at what they do. There is speculation that in some sectors – the digital economy is usually given as an example – a smaller group of top firms experience "a winner takes all" situation. For some industries this may be linked to power law dynamics, where a small change in one variable creates a bigger change in another. More negatively, in terms of real productivity growth there is some evidence that those at the very top can benefit by exploiting a degree of monopoly power by creating bigger mark-ups. Given the arguments about the role of globalization and the development of integrated supply chains in modern capitalism, it is also not surprising to find that, even allowing for doubts about the data, foreign-owned firms and plants tend to be more productive than domestically owned ones. There may be an easier transmission of new technologies, organizational improvements and ideas across national borders at the top rather than down the ladder of uneven performance *within* economies.

Despite hopes that regional differences would diminish as economies became more highly developed, they too seem to be an intractable part of productivity variation globally. Capital cities, for example, tend to attract the types of activity that generate high levels of productivity and higher incomes for their inhabitants. Beyond them the situation is often less happy. In the past regional patterns might have been explained by access to raw materials, things like coal and iron. But fewer industries today are tied to place in this way. Still, "path dependency" is hard to change. This gives the debate over regional productivity gaps and income levels an additional degree of angst and political resonance.

There is another part of this debate on productivity unevenness that is important. This is the question of the comparative productivity of the state and private sectors. Recent economic thinking, at least until the crash of 2008, has been dominated by the idea that private enterprises have higher productivity than state enterprises. For some this is a matter of faith. The evidence is less compelling. Separating private and state is not easy. There is a significant grey area of hybrid state/private organizations. Even in the seemingly more "private" part of the private sector, while state support of "lame duck" companies is often disparaged its essential role in other private sector successes is often, as we have seen, downplayed.

States have tended to take over private enterprises in two situations: when they act as de facto public monopolies and when private companies have been manifestly failing. The latter might be a product of a short-term crisis (as with parts of the banking system in 2008). More often it has been the product of sectoral decline and structural shift. This clearly creates a problem for any productivity comparison. So too does the way that successful state-owned companies might be sold off to the private sector. Beyond this, nationalized industries were, and still are, often hampered by government policies and restrictions not placed on private enterprises. Some critics have gone further and argued that to make the case for privatization stronger the position of some state firms has been deliberately weakened. It is all the more telling that studies which have looked at the comparative productivity performance of state and privately owned firms struggle to show big differences. Nor is it clear that performance improved after privatization. The post-privatization record in the UK, for example, looks even poorer if account is taken of the way that privatization processes have often been structured to secure higher levels of subsidy or profits by guaranteed price increases. It is not surprising to find that some privatizations have been reversed in some countries. The state bad/private good productivity argument becomes stranger still given that some state companies have effectively become multinationals so that, for example, Britain's privatized train operators are in fact still largely state owned: by the French, Dutch and German states for example, just not (mostly) by the British state.

If this argument about the role of the private sector, markets and the state in productivity growth in the advanced world is still very real, it is even more central to the debates about how some poorer countries have achieved growth and productivity miracles in more recent decades.

# 6

# Miracle productivity growth in the Asian Tigers?

What is the story in the larger part of the world where productivity has risen but not so much as to allow the types of gains that have created the wealth of the developed world? In this chapter we are going to focus on three cases: South Korea, China and India. They each started late and had different degrees of success in raising their productivity; so much so that they are sometimes seen as examples of miracle productivity growth. But first we need to put their stories into the wider perspective of the global productivity pattern.

Most of the high-productivity economies today are members of the OECD. It was formed in 1961 as a "Western" group in the midst of the Cold War. Today it has 36 members with an average per capita nominal income of some $41,000. Unfortunately, the population of the OECD countries today makes up only 17 per cent of the world's population. High productivity is not an explicit membership requirement of the OECD. Politics matters too. This explains why Russia is still not a member. But the high productivity of the OECD economies makes them a huge force in the global economy. In Asia only Japan and South Korea are members. In Central and South America only Chile and Mexico. No African country is a member of the OECD.

Table 6.1 shows the productivity gaps which exist today. We are again measuring these in terms of GDP per person employed because the poorer economies lack good enough data to calculate GDP per hour worked. Some regional categories are ragbag ones. There is a big gap, for example, between the economies with oil in the Middle East and North Africa and those without it. Still, the contrasts are sharp. We see here the leading role of the US and the relatively high position of the OECD as a whole, even allowing for some members with weaker productivity levels. The five BRICS are a coming together of Brazil, Russia, India, China and South Africa. The BRICS countries have size – their combined population amounts to 42 per cent of the global population – but their average nominal GDP per capita is just under \$7,000. They are also far from moving forwards at the same speed and their performance and level is dominated by China. Their average productivity level is low to middling. Below them are the peoples of the rest of the world whose lives are still moulded by very low productivity levels even if these have advanced somewhat in recent decades.

**Table 6.1** Global labour productivity levels: GDP, 2017

|  | US (%) | OECD average (%) |
|---|---|---|
| US | 100 | 135 |
| OECD | 74 | 100 |
| BRICS with official China | 22 | 30 |
| BRICS with unofficial China | 20 | 27 |
| Middle East and North Africa | 51 | 70 |
| Russia and rest ex-Soviet bloc | 40 | 54 |
| Latin America | 28 | 38 |
| China official | 25 | 34 |
| China unofficial | 21 | 27 |
| India | 14 | 20 |
| Other developing Asia | 17 | 23 |
| Sub-Saharan Africa | 8 | 11 |

*Source*: Author's calculations from US Conference Board.

### Tracking the changes

Where do South Korea, China and India fit in? We saw in the last chapter that the foundations of Japan's postwar progress were laid well before 1939. If we leave aside the smaller Asian economies like Hong Kong and Singapore, then the most successful post-1945 economy to close the productivity gap has been South Korea. China began to move later and then, even more belatedly, India. Figure 6.1 takes us back to the grand sweep of global economy history over the last 2,000 years.

We can see that in the pre-capitalist era, what are modern-day China, India and Korea were all more advanced than Europe and its offshoots (measured here by the US level). But they fell back in relative terms as capitalist industrialization took off. Whereas Europe clearly benefited from

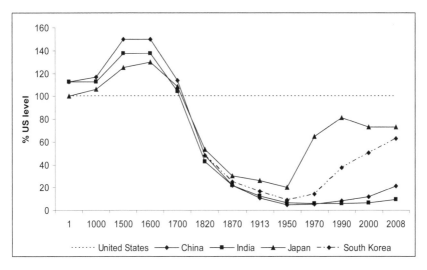

**Figure 6.1** Output per head in China, India, Japan and South Korea as a percentage of US level

*Source*: Maddison database.

being able to draw on the globe for its productivity rise, the impact on the rest of the world was more dubious. Everywhere it involved a "brutal rupture and reorientation ... one of the most far-reaching, brutal ruptures in modern history" (Hall 2017). India and China are interesting cases. Unlike in Japan the disruptive nature of the links with Europe began to manifest themselves much earlier. In the Indian subcontinent, the British East India Company, formed in 1600, became ever more powerful in the eighteenth century and effectively ruled "India" as a whole from 1818 until 1858. Following the 1857 Indian mutiny, "India" became a formal crown colony until its independence in 1947. China was never formally colonized, but economic distortion began in the nineteenth century and with it came political interference and the carving out of treaty ports under European control. The results were neither an advertisement for formal and informal empire nor for globalization. Output per head does seem to have increased in India by some 25 per cent between 1820 and 1913. In China it may have fallen by just under 10 per cent. Then in the interwar years India may have seen a fall and China the tiniest of increases. This has not stopped those who believe in the romance of productivity trying to accentuate the positive. Such claims can be put into perspective by noting that the overall shares of global output produced in China and India fell from 49 per cent in 1820 to 18 per cent in 1938.

Figure 6.1 also shows the catch-up that has occurred since 1945. It also points us to the danger of ignoring differences. South Korea has made the jump to an advanced society. China has picked up but still has a long way to go and India has even further. We can trace some indicators of the changes since 1945 in Table 6.2, which uses more recent data and adds the urbanization share.

**Table 6.2** Economic and urban growth (%), 1950–2018

|         | Per capita income, 2011$ | | | Urban (%) | | |
|---------|-------------|-------|-------|-------------|-------|-------|
|         | South Korea | China | India | South Korea | China | India |
| 1950    | 1,178       | 637   | 824   | 21.4        | 11.8  | 17.0  |
| 1960    | 1,691       | 843   | 1,002 | 27.7        | 16.2  | 17.9  |
| 1970    | 2,989       | 1,115 | 1,155 | 40.7        | 17.4  | 19.8  |
| 1980    | 5,674       | 1,539 | 1,249 | 56.7        | 19.4  | 23.1  |
| 1990    | 12,004      | 2,379 | 1,742 | 73.8        | 26.4  | 25.5  |
| 2000    | 21,420      | 4,202 | 2,505 | 79.6        | 35.9  | 27.7  |
| 2010    | 31,321      | 9,555 | 4,487 | 81.9        | 49.2  | 30.9  |
| 2016–15 | 36,103      | 12,569| 6,215 | 81.6        | 55.5  | 32.8  |

*Source*: Groningen Growth and Development Centre; World Urbanization Prospects.

Note that South Korea moves forwards quite fast from early on. China starts lower down than India but even during the Maoist period its early growth was faster so it caught up. (There are different data sets available and some do not believe China made as much progress before the late 1970s as is shown here.) Then, from the 1980s, the beginnings of reform in the Chinese economy help it to surge forwards. India's growth occurs later and, while better than in Latin America or Africa, it has not been as strong or consistent as that of China (Basu 2018). Table 6.2 also enables us to be more precise about the size of the gaps that still need to be closed. The urbanization shares are particularly important in giving us a sense of these gaps. South Korea has been an urban society for a generation, China for a few years, while over two-thirds of the Indian population still live in the India "of the villages".

Can we believe these and more detailed productivity statistics for these societies? We know that the problems of productivity data are worse in

poorer societies and that they are compounded when economies grow rap-
idly. Additionally, in the case of China, it is often argued that enterprises
inflate their results to please the centre. "During a five-minute talk with the
government, many enterprises, spend the first three minutes bragging and
the last two kissing ass", said Jack Ma of Alibaba (quoted in *China Report*,
June 2019). Two figures are given for China's average productivity level in
Table 6.1: an official one and an estimated one some 15 per cent lower. None
of this can detract from the huge advance that has been made. The rising urbanization share (there are some measurement problems here too)
is evidence enough for this. But Indian data are also controversial, with
some arguing that they overstate the pace of change there (Subramanian
2019). These doubts are another reason to be sceptical of some of the more
"sophisticated" quantitative analysis of Chinese and Indian productivity and
its growth.

The bigger the Chinese economy becomes, the more significant it is as
a global player. With a population four times the size of that of the United
States, even with an output per head 25 per cent lower than the US level it
will equal it in size. As China grows it is also playing a bigger role in global
growth and the rising level of global productivity. Since the global crisis
of 2008 we have seen that the richest economies have performed weakly
and their productivity growth has been poor. In China, instead of pulling
back, the authorities drove the economy forwards so that its share of global
growth has risen even more. In more normal years, though, because Chinese
growth is faster its share of global growth is still around 25–30 per cent. If
China falters then so too will the global economy.

Overcoming low productivity in our three economies has opened up the
prospect of rising standards of living. Globally the share of people living in
extreme poverty (less than $1.90 a day is the current extreme poverty line)
has fallen. Poverty data, like productivity data, are controversial. There are
sharp debates about the extent to which there is real improvement or the
use of "statistical theatre" to create the illusion of greater progress (Hickel
2017). But a significant, if disputed, part of the real global progress is due to
the poverty reducing productivity growth in China. Before 2005 China had
a higher share of its population living in extreme poverty than the global
average. Since then its share has been below the global average and today it
is around only 2 per cent. In China the rural population remains the poorest
part of the populace, but it has moved forwards too. But a better life is to be

**Table 6.3** Estimates of percentage share of Chinese urban households with different income levels

| Type of consumer | Income | 2000 | 2010 | 2020 |
|---|---|---|---|---|
| Poor | < $6,000 | 36 | 10 | 7 |
| Value | $6,000–16,000 | 63 | 83 | 36 |
| Mainstream | $16,000–34.000 | 1 | 6 | 51 |
| Affluent | $34,000+ | – | 2 | 6 |

*Source*: McKinsey (2012: 14).

found in the towns, and every year people move officially and unofficially on a massive scale.

Table 6.3 shows the estimates made by the McKinsey organization regarding how urban households are distributed by income level. The precision of the data may be spurious but the scale and rapidity of the change is obvious even if, hidden in the data, there is the distortion of the emergence of a powerful billionaire group at the very top.

## The components of miracle productivity growth

When we break down the basic ingredients of the East Asian success stories, they have some important elements in common with the seemingly failed Soviet model. Just as in the USSR at its peak, the successful economies have mobilized resources on a massive scale. Their growth has involved a massive amount of sweat. Such resource mobilization may not guarantee success but the lack of it will almost certainly guarantee failure. What were the resources that were being piled in? The answer is some (improved) land and an awful lot of labour with improved educational levels and a huge amount of capital.

South Korea, China and India have all faced limits on expanding the land input. The land input in India has been more or less constant for the last half century, that in China rose in the 1980s but then stabilized. But the quality of land has been improved through better land use, irrigation, fertilizers, etc. Here China has been much more successful than India.

The role of labour has been clearer. Labour force participation rates have been pushed up. A high birth rate and greater survival rates produce a younger labour force which some claim is positive for productivity growth. China has "benefited" less because of its attempts to control population.

**Table 6.4** Educational attainment in Korea, China and India, for population 15+

|      | Average years of schooling | | | % with no schooling | | |
|------|-------------|-------|-------|-------------|-------|-------|
|      | South Korea | China | India | South Korea | China | India |
| 1960 | 4.7         | 2.5   | 1.4   | 40          | 56    | 72    |
| 1980 | 8.3         | 4.4   | 2.9   | 14          | 32    | 56    |
| 2000 | 11.1        | 6.0   | 4.5   | 8           | 16    | 43    |

*Source*: Bosworth and Collins (2008: 52).

But it seems likely that the bigger gains have come from improvements in labour quality through greater literacy, mass schooling and the development of secondary and higher education. Table 6.4 shows the impressive gains in our three societies.

The Asian success stories also all involve high rates of savings and investment supplemented by different amounts of foreign direct investment. Even today, South Korea sustains the highest share of capital investment in the OECD. Chinese growth has been driven, too, by high levels of capital investment. India has failed to match either case, although its record is still positive. Not the least important thing here is that productivity growth comes from not only having more capital but better capital: better infrastructure, better buildings, better tools and equipment within them and better knowledge and organization to use them.

But it is not sufficient to put more in, you also need to improve the way you use your resources, and that includes massive technological and organizational change, which means "borrowing". "Late industrialisation was a case of pure learning, meaning total dependence on other countries' commercialised technology to establish modern industries" (Amsden 2001: 1). This policy has been quite conscious. The governments of South Korea and China especially have had a clear sense of the importance of knowledge transfer. They have sent people abroad to learn. They have used freely available knowledge. They have acquired knowledge embodied in purchased machinery (including purchases of second-hand machinery) and capital goods. And they have also "stolen" knowledge in defiance of the increasingly restrictive intellectual property rights regime.

Not only were inputs increased but their allocation has been changing away from low-productivity sectors to higher-productivity ones through our old friend structural change. A crude indicator of structural change can be seen in the urbanization shares shown in Table 6.2. This has had a substantial impact on the overall productivity rate. In China, for example, at the turn of the 1980s productivity in the non-agricultural sector is estimated to have been some six times higher than in the agricultural sector, so it is easy to see the big gains that began to come with structural change.

## Productivity growth in the different sectors

We saw in Chapter 1 that the rise in agricultural productivity in the last 50 years has been a major event in world history. In our miracle economies, its rise has been remarkable too but their performance has differed. In the 1960s India had the agricultural productivity edge over China. Since then China has significantly outperformed India. Yields per acre are higher and, as incomes have risen, it has been able to switch towards higher-value crops and animal farming. Labour productivity figures point in the same direction. The key difference is not plot size. That has been falling in India but in China it is still smaller. Nor is it fertilizer inputs or even seeds. Superior Chinese agricultural productivity growth seems to depend more on investment, not least in irrigation and infrastructure financed in one form or another by the Chinese state.

Productivity growth has been faster still in industry and services. But there is a major difference between the pattern in China (and South Korea before it) and that in India. It is the manufacturing prowess of South Korea and now China that, following Japan, seems to stand out. Starting with relatively simple goods, they have moved up the international division of labour to produce much more complex manufactured goods, albeit at different levels. However, the share of labour in manufacturing has *not* risen to anything like the same levels achieved in Europe in the 1950s. If we take individual examples then in Japan it seems that the percentage of the labour force in industry peaked in 1973 at 37 per cent and for South Korea it peaked around 1991 at the same level, where it is now under 25 per cent. Part of the explanation is that the levels of productivity in manufacturing are now so high that they require fewer inputs, not least of labour. We are yet to fully understand the implications of this peaking of the manufacturing share at much lower levels for countries that are trying to catch up with the productivity levels of the OECD bloc. High manufacturing productivity means that labour can be released for other things: the Baumol effect again. The problem is, what are those other things? What we do know is that workers move from the countryside to the cities less to work in factories than to work in service jobs of one kind or another. But at least there was a manufacturing surge in South Korea and in China. In India the manufacturing sector has not grown by anything like the same extent.

Some argue that this is not a problem. An Indian "networked" service economy can leapfrog over the need for a high-productivity manufacturing industry and others, not least in Africa, can follow in its wake. The attraction of having a high-productivity services sector built, for example, around finance and business processing is easy to see. But high-productivity/ high-value services are the lesser part of any service sector. Services everywhere are overwhelmingly about doing the basic stuff. NASSCOM, the Indian trade association for business process outsourcing, claims that the numbers directly employed in this sector have risen from 0.4 million in 2001 to 2 million in 2008 and 3.9 million in 2017. However, the promised outsourcing boom to India has proved less dramatic than some imagined. Some tasks outsourced to India have been moved back to Europe, others moved on to new countries. India's English-speaking population is of no help in attracting work from non-English seeking countries. Worse, while 10 per cent of Indians are said to speak English, most do so as a second or third language with questionable levels of fluency. The percentage able to do high-level work is much lower. Indeed, there do not seem to be enough jobs for English speakers. This is one reason why there has also been a diversion of "talented" Indians towards international computer fraud, another example of Baumol's destructive entrepreneurship (Poonam 2019). Just as in manufacturing supply chains, so in service ones a disproportionate gain also goes to the advanced world. Some suggest a 4:1 split for services. The significance of any gain in Indian higher-level service work, no less than the gain in China and elsewhere for manufacturing, is not to be sneered at, but neither can the unequal distribution of the gains be ignored.

There is another way of thinking about sectors. This is the division between the formal and the informal sector characterized by casual labour and underemployment. Productivity will therefore be low and the output share much less than the labour force share. Some economists argue that for the centre of gravity of the economy to be in the higher-productivity formal sector then the informal sector must not be responsible for more than 30 per cent of GDP. The figure in South Korea is lower. In China it is higher, but exactly where is much harder to answer. The figure in India is huge: some say 90 per cent of the labour force is informally employed. A focus on any bright new factories and offices should not obscure the massive scale of informal employment and its productivity complications.

## How were they able to do it?

In Chapter 2 we argued that thinking of productivity in terms of the addition of more inputs and greater efficiency in their use through technological and organizational change is of limited help. Nor are those accounts that use a production function growth-accounting framework any better. We need to know how these elements were combined and why it was easier to get a combination that worked better in some places than in others.

When we explore this, we can begin by dismissing those accounts which claim that "culture" is the key. It is certainly necessary to engage with the real history of societies, but this is not what "culturalist accounts" tend to do. When Samuel Huntington tried to understand how cultural-civilizational elements underpinned the world's economic and political fault lines, he could not decide whether the important elements of culture were religious (Islam, Confucianism, Hinduism, etc.), national (Japanese, Chinese, etc.), regional (European, Asian, African, etc.) or civilizational ("Western", "Eastern", etc.). Culturalist accounts stumble too on whether the issue is culture in some abstract, high-culture sense, or culture as it is popularly experienced. In either case, too often the discussion becomes a projection of one's own imagined values against the values of an imaginary "other". Then there is the question of the direction of any change. Max Weber tried to offer an account of Protestantism *leading* to the rise of the West, but it could just as easily be seen as a consequence. Those who have tried to apply the same logic to the "East" have suffered the same fate. When the economies of East Asia appeared stuck in poverty, the culturalists claimed that it was down to negative "Asian values". When productivity surged, the culture explanation flipped to stress the same values as positive "Asian" ones.

When we focus on the economic dimension, the discussion of the miracle economies takes us straight to the heart of the debate about development policy. For a generation after 1945 there seemed to be widespread agreement that markets needed to be directed by states, especially where development was concerned. The argument was over the degree of state direction, and this became tied up with Cold War issues, not least for the newly independent states that were forced to take sides. From the late 1970s, however, there was a huge shift in ideas and policy, especially in the West. The Soviet model now looked less attractive, and when poorer countries began to be hit by debt crises the argument was that these were in part a product of excessive statism. Most poorer countries had squandered the chances of productivity revolutions by using overly prescriptive and inward-looking policies. The result was economic failure, corruption and political repression. These arguments were re-enforced by international policy reflected in the so-called Washington Consensus. This was a set of policies supported by the US, the IMF, the World Bank and the World Trade Organization (WTO, created in 1995). Ironically, in many parts of the world where more pro-market policies were used, the results were even worse, but to maintain the view that these were the way forward it became common to claim that their success could be seen in the progress of a group of Asian Tigers that included South Korea. China and India were then added as they deregulated their economies, looked to integrate into the world economy and so, it is claimed, unleashed a new dynamism.

Over time this story of productivity advance (and policy advice) came to focus on a 4P approach:

Productivity = f (Prices, Profits, Property)

The first requirement for productivity to rise is to have the right *prices*. This means prices that are formed by the invisible hand of the market (largely excluding the externality issue). With the right prices, businesses in the private sector can then use the second P – *profit* – to inform their decisions. Chasing profit for the private sector is trickier because businesses can easily be seduced into forms of rent seeking. However, since most of the rent-seeking opportunities arise from the role of the state, keeping the state as small as possible helps to reduce this problem.

In the 1980s and 1990s many economists seemed to take the view that all that was needed to enhance productivity was "getting prices right" and allowing the profit motive to work. The argument that this was what was happening in the first East Asian cases was embodied in a 1993 report by the World Bank, *The East Asian Miracle*. China had already begun to move after the death of Mao in 1976 and the decision of Deng Xiaoping and his supporters in 1978/9 that the way forward was less state, more market and greater integration with the global economy, including joining the WTO in 2001. The same applied to India, whose policy shift to deregulation began in 1991, just as the 1993 World Bank report was being put together. "India grows at night, when the state sleeps", has become a popular view of its progress since then.

The 1993 report was a brave effort to claim productivity growth in these economies as market miracles. But few were convinced and failures elsewhere seemed to loom large and undermine confidence that all that was necessary was "getting prices right" and reducing the role of the state to unleash the dynamism of the profit motive. As these arguments came under sustained criticism an additional element was added to the argument. This is our third input P: *property*. Prices and profits will only come together in a positive way if the right property relations and the right institutions to support them are in place.

Today much of the debate on how to get productivity growth in poor countries is based on arguments about property and institutions. Economists like Acemoglu and Robinson argue that "countries differ in their success because of their different institutions" (Acemoglu & Robinson 2012: 73). "Extractive states" hold productivity and growth down by encouraging rent seeking. Inclusive states open up potential by spreading power and creating new possibilities. Unfortunately, getting the right state and the right property relations is not easy. History and path dependency seem important. But which history? Critics argue that these accounts sacrifice complexity in favour of stylized facts which are used to support "just so stories". This idea refers to Rudyard Kipling's fairy tales about how, for example, the elephant got his trunk, rather than real histories. "Just so" institutionalism is gilded with a few real "facts" and data crunched to support the 4P conclusion, an approach brutally dismissed by Branko Milanovic as "Wikipedia with regressions" (quoted in Jerven 2015: 73).

There is an even bigger problem. Assume for the moment that the focus on markets is right. On any account the visible hand of the Chinese state continues to play an important role. Yet China has done better than India. One way that supporters of the 4P approach get around this is to insist that the role of the state in China is exaggerated. Others argue that an even greater dynamism will soon be unleashed in "market" India whereas "statist" China is heading for a fall unless it reforms more. (The implication is also that had China been more market-oriented, it would have done even better.) This latter view is supported by Acemoglu and Robinson. The dead weight of the extractive state will sooner or later be reflected in the productivity figures. It is already evident in the problems of inefficiency in parts of the economy where resources are misallocated and huge debts have been built up, leading to China having its zombie firms like those in the West.

Predictions of a Chinese fall have been made for several decades. It has not happened yet. The history of past productivity growth does suggest that there are problems in sustaining it. Economies can stumble in what some call "middle-income development traps", getting so far and then finding a loss of dynamism. But this does not mean that these traps cannot be negotiated. South Korea (and Japan before it) showed this and China may show it in the future.

There is a quite different story regarding how these economies have been and are driving productivity and growth forwards. A significant group of economists argue that the success is as much a product of continued state action as the market. The 4P approach is a myth. These economies did not "get prices right". They often got them wrong, sometimes quite deliberately, and it worked. Nor did they depend on a simple profit drive. They did not look to maximize their immediate position in the international division of labour but to improve it over the longer term. This might have meant short-term inefficiency losses but it led to longer-term gains: the problem we identified in Chapter 2. They certainly integrated more into the global economy but they also controlled that integration and directed it. Rather than slavishly follow the rules of the Washington Consensus, they either openly rejected them or subverted and bent them.

There is no single view within this group. One of its leading proponents is Alice Amsden. Another is Robert Wade. Ha-Joon Chang, born in South Korea, has also been a prominent voice arguing that neither the past successes of growth in earlier times nor those of today have been based on "textbook models". We might also include more mainstream economists like Dani Rodrik, who argues that creative industrial policies are a vital part of any productivity and growth agenda. Table 6.5 is drawn from Rodrik's own account and sets out the main differences between what he believes to be the real pattern of Asian success stories and the imagined one.

**Table 6.5** Dani Rodrik's East Asian pattern

| Institutional domain | Standard ideal | East Asian pattern |
| --- | --- | --- |
| 1. Property rights | Private, enforced by rule of law | Private but government authority can override law |
| 2. Corporate governance | Shareholder ("outsider") control, protection of shareholder rights | Insider control |
| 3. Business–government relations | Arms' length rules based | Close interactions |
| 4. Industrial organization | Decentralized competitive markets with tough anti-trust | Horizontal and vertical integration; government-supported cartels |
| 5. Financial system | Deregulated, securities based, with free entry; prudential supervision through regulatory oversight | Bank based, restricted entry, heavily controlled by government, directed lending, weak formal regulation |
| 6. Labour markets | Decentralised, deinstitutionalised, "flexible" labour markets | Lifetime employment in core enterprise (Japan) |
| 7. International capital flows | "Prudently" free | Restricted until 1990s |
| 8. Public ownership | None in productive sectors | Plenty in upstream sectors |

*Source*: Rodrik (2005: 976).

This approach can also help us make better sense of the Indian experience. One big problem with the conventional focus on deregulation from 1991 is that the Indian economy had already started growing faster in the 1980s. There is debate too about the extent of reforms and their impact. As in the West, pro-market accounts often neglect the "entrepreneurial role of the state". In India, Bangalore, for example, did not by chance become the IT city. In 1972 it was picked as the location for the Indian Space Research Organization. This made it a natural centre for subsequent IT-based growth and partly explains why leading Indian companies like Infosys and Wipro located there and why some multinationals also found it an attractive location.

This focus still leaves the question of what enabled a developmentalist state to work better in some cases than in others. Here there is some overlap with the other institutionalist arguments but, as is evident from Rodrik's table, there is not the same focus on the sacrosanct nature of private property. The ability of the state to mobilize is in part explained by the fact that inequalities were constrained so that it was less a prisoner of private interests and more able to manoeuvre internally and externally. Methodologically these accounts differ too in that they try to more sensitively reconstruct the recent economic history of these countries rather than crunch numbers to play more games of "Wikipedia with regressions".

These accounts also point to something else: the importance of what has been called "the development space" (Wade 2003). This refers to the external room for manoeuvre that economies have in the global economy. Economic possibilities vary over time. Export-led growth depends on a positive external environment. It is dependent too on the technologies available. The more recent extension of supply chains needed not only information technology but more basic innovations like the productivity gains that came with containerization.

The development space also exists in terms of ideas and policy. Ha-Joon Chang has followed the nineteenth-century economist Friedrich List in arguing that richer countries use their superior power to "kick away the ladder" for poorer ones by foisting free market policies on them. Just as Alexander Hamilton was wise to reject this for the US in the nineteenth century, so today the success cases in East Asia were wise to reject it in the twentieth century and beyond (Chang 2002).

The development space is also set geopolitically. Both Japan and South Korea benefited from their roles as valuable Western allies in the Cold War. They were the recipients of considerable assistance. Hindering their exports did not seem a wise move either, if they needed to be kept on board. India was in a more ambiguous position and China was clearly on "the other side", even if it had fallen out with the USSR and was to some degree being wooed by the US. Nevertheless, it too met a relatively benign external environment in the 1990s and 2000s.

Today this is less so. China is seen as more of a threat and a potentially dangerous competitor, and as a more determined regional power and possibly a future global one. This brings antagonisms and more demands for military spending on all sides. Governments and companies in more advanced areas are taking a less benign view of its economic rise. We may now be moving towards a world in which a once more belligerent USA is looking askance at China as a potential challenger and trying to close down the space for its future development and others who might want to emulate it. Such policies predated the Trump presidency but his explicit "America first" rhetoric made the direction of policy more obvious.

This does not augur well for productivity revolutions in poorer countries either. They too might become victims of a more hostile policy climate. But they also face in China an economy out of all proportion to any other save India. The question of whether China's rise is closing down the space for others is one we will have to return to.

### How far can China's and India's productivity levels rise?

The experience of South Korea shows that even big productivity gaps can be closed in a relatively short period of time. With a population of some 51 million, it is now ranked around 22 in terms of nominal GDP per capita and, as we have seen, it has made it to the OECD. But we must beware of thinking that two economies with over a quarter of the world's population have the internal and external potential to do the same. Many, although not necessarily China's and India's rulers, think they cannot.

We ought now to be able to agree that some slowdown will inevitably come at some point because we know that productivity growth is S-shaped. We cannot project any significant economic indicator forwards forever in a straight line. South Korea's own trajectory shows this, as did that of Japan and every successful economy before them. As the gaps close and the boost from structural change is lost, then growth rates as a whole, and productivity increases within them, will reduce. However, both China and India still have some way to go. Beyond this, views get more controversial.

One possibility is that the growth of productivity of China and India will have to slow down – perhaps they will even choose to slow down – because of the negative environmental and wider ecological load that this is creating. Although per capita levels of resource use are still less than in the advanced societies, they *are* rising, meaning that China in particular is becoming an even more important importer of food and resources to feed its population and economy. So far as negative outputs are concerned, both countries are notorious for their pollution levels. In recent years China has sought to try to deal with this and now proclaims its green potential. It is even a major exporter of solar panels, which can reduce both the fossil energy input and pollution and global warming output. But it still has a long way to go. India has barely begun to address the problem.

Of course, the bad side of productivity growth is not purely an internal issue. It is also affected by planetary limits. Yet it is unlikely that these economies will voluntarily relinquish the chances of further growth even if they are taking environmental issues more seriously. To agree to slow down for these reasons would require a very different set of priorities globally. It would also require a very different set of internal priorities.

Further productivity growth could be held back by related international tensions. In the case of China (and to a lesser extent India), the measures taken by the US are designed to hinder further advance by forcing it to rely more on its own internally generated progress. The hope is then, for some in the US, that China might economically go the same way as the USSR. Whether it does, depends in part on whether any sanctions can be successfully enforced and how far China has already advanced if it needs to become a more self-sustaining innovation hub.

From the 1960s onwards manufacturing production began to shift from the more highly productive economies to the less productive ones where labour was cheaper. The activity in the most productive economies became more focused on high-level, knowledge-intensive elements of production and services. Global productivity then rose because some poor countries now benefited from the productivity effects of manufacturing growth. But these countries still remain lower down the international order. They are moving forwards but rather, some argue, like birds in formation. Sustained movement up the international division of labour is not easy. Value-added levels in China are still modest. The iPhone, *assembled* in China, is a well-known example. The biggest value elements in Chinese exports are often embodied in components that were previously imported.

A key characteristic of the South Korean experience, and more recently that of China, is that there seems to have been an understanding that beyond a certain point it is also necessary to move towards generating your own inventions, innovations, designs, etc. The USSR had tried this, but because of the Cold War it could not officially import high technology and the focus of research and development tended to be on the military sector. Similar pressures exist in the Asian cases, but growth in South Korea and China has also stressed the civilian sectors. South Korea has had some success. Samsung challenges Apple in the high-end smartphone market. I drive one of the 8 per cent of cars currently being bought in the UK from a South Korean company.

The situation for China is less clear. One of President Xi's goals has been to make the economy more sophisticated. Chinese research and development expenditure has risen impressively from 0.7 per cent of GDP in 1991 (not untypical for a poorer country) to 1.9 per cent in 2012. Despite not being as developed, China had hit the OECD average. Since then it has exceeded it. The number of patents in China is another measure: this figure "has exploded" too. Unfortunately, not everything that is important is patented and patents measure claimed "invention" more than actual "innovation". Patent levels also vary between sectors and their originality and quality are often unclear. Still, it is hard not to be impressed by their rising numbers and their seeming quality. The big improvement in China, says one analysis, is "real and robust", although China has still a long way to go to close the wider technology and productivity gap (Wei *et al.* 2017; Siyi & Ying 2019).

What has been achieved so far makes China look not only impressive but a possible model for emulation. In productivity discussion politics is never far away. The economic base on which power lies in international politics is:

People × Productivity = Power

Once you have power then you can also project the stories that you want people to accept. China is moving outwards. Japan did this disastrously in the 1930s then more circumspectly in the second half of the twentieth century. South Korea, too, has a global presence. But China's rise is creating much bigger waves. It needs to draw on the world for resources and markets. It is also part of the network of global interstate competition. This involves both military competition and competition for influence, in which aid, investment and ideas all play a role

One idea that has gained popularity is that China is offering an alternative "Beijing Consensus" to the ideas endorsed by Washington and the major international institutions. The idea of a Beijing consensus emerged more from popular commentary in the West than serious analysis. But within China there is talk of a Chinese model to project to others as an alternative. China claims that it is not tarred with the brush of imperialism and neocolonialism. It has been a victim itself, its productivity held back by the disruption and negative relations they imposed before 1948. Now, having emancipated itself from both the more distant and more recent past, it has unleashed its potential in a way that others can follow. China's huge "belt and road" initiative, through which it is trying to improve infrastructure across Asia and beyond, is an example of this. There is clearly self-interest here: it boosts China's economy and trade, but there is also the argument about unlocking productivity change on a wider scale. Beyond the "belt and road" states, China also appears as a significant aid giver, investor and partner in other parts of Asia, Africa, Latin America and even Europe. Here too there is self-interest, but if China has the secret of the success and if it is willing to help you unblock your productivity problems, then why not accept its aid and advice? In Chapter 7 we will look at sub-Saharan Africa and the role of China there, but before we do there is one more big issue to discuss. This is the role of authoritianism in productivity growth.

## Productivity: top down or bottom up?

The argument for more statist approaches to realize productivity gains tends to come from the political Left. But there is a problem. The "successes" in Asia have all involved a degree of "labour repression". People have been forced to make sacrifices now in order to make gains later. Coercion has always been part of the story of productivity growth. Productivity change has, more often than not, been imposed from the top down. Eventually something gives and protests explode, as happened successfully in South Korea but unsuccessfully in China in 1989. The question is, does labour repression have to be part of productivity growth in the future? This is not just a question for people in these countries. The integration of supply chains across the globe means that we are all beneficiaries of productivity miracles that may involve more coercion than we like to think about.

As late as 1985, Paul Samuelson was asking students in his classic textbook whether political repression in Russia was "worth the economic gains", and suggesting that this question was "one of the most profound dilemmas in human society" (quoted in Ebenstein 2015: 185). The collapse of the USSR merely refocused the question. It is at the heart of the comparative evaluation of India and China. Amartya Sen is famous for the argument that the famines which have killed millions are characteristic of undemocratic societies. Indian himself, his key example is the disappearance of famine in that country *after* it became independent of British rule. But the comparison also had a contemporary thrust. Famines disappeared in India after 1947 but China had a huge one in 1959–61. Like the USSR it also had episodes of severe mass repression. Estimates put the numbers of excess deaths in several tens of millions. In India, on the other hand, democracy reduced repression, it reduced the factors that caused famine and it led to the threat of famine being recognized early on.

Case closed? Not quite. Sen also noted that in 1947 India and China had very similar levels of infant mortality, death rates and life expectancy. Then even before the 1980s, China's marginally superior productivity growth led to its death rates falling faster than those in India. Today, as far as morbidity, mortality and longevity are concerned, South Korea has a large and decisive lead over both, and China has a large lead over India. Table 6.6 shows the Human Development Index scores.

South Korea is way ahead. We can see the significant improvement in "democratic" India, but also how far behind "authoritarian" China it still is. In 2018 life expectancy at birth was 82.4 years in South Korea. In China it was 76.4 and only 68.8 in India. Writing in 1989, Sen did a back-of-the-envelope calculation that in the proceeding years India's excess of deaths over China had been 4 million a year. "India seems to manage to fill its cupboard with more skeletons every eight years than China put there in its years of shame", he and his co-author wrote (Dreze & Sen 1990: 215).

**Table 6.6** The benefits of productivity growth? Human Development Index (HDI) rankings

|      | HDI index | | | | Global HDI ranking | | |
|------|-------|-------------|-------|-------|-------------|-------|-------|
|      | World | South Korea | China | India | South Korea | China | India |
| 1990 | 0.598 | 0.728 | 0.502 | 0.427 | 37  | 131 | 148 |
| 2000 | 0.644 | 0.817 | 0.594 | 0.493 | 29  | 120 | 139 |
| 2010 | 0.698 | 0.884 | 0.706 | 0.581 | 23  | 99  | 134 |
| 2017 | 0.728 | 0.903 | 0.752 | 0.640 | 23= | 86  | 130 |

Source: Compiled by author from United Nations Human Development reports.

The China–India contrast is the most obvious example of the problem of the controversial link between productivity and politics. It would be naive to imagine that this issue does not appear elsewhere. Many economists take the view that productivity needs to be driven up by technocratic means over the heads of people. This is reflected in the attitudes in the international financial institutions. It is even built into the indices they devise to compare the economic climates of different countries. Measures to increase equality, and to bring greater social welfare and justice, often appear as bureaucratic and red-tape hindrances to business and productivity. The World Bank's *Doing Business Report* had to withdraw a component which ranked countries down for having minimum wages, paid overtime and holidays, and redundancy pay (Hickel 2017: 215). Similarly, the logic of the much critical economic discussion of China is less that its people need more democratic control in the economy as well as politics, than that state economic power needs to be converted into private economic power through privatization. What has been called the "China price" – low wages and poor conditions – would continue. Privatization would just make "legitimate" what was "illegitimate" when done by the state.

We can see this thinking too in those economic discussions which claim to identify the virtuous circles that come from having the right institutions connecting property and politics to productivity. Too often these leave vague the questions of which institutions matter and how they were or are to be achieved. Acemoglu and Robinson's account never clearly defines and details the institutions that matter, and their arguments about how they come into being seem largely to revolve around contingency and path dependency. There is no capitalism here, and there is colonialism but no imperialism (which rather lets the US off the hook). There is a limited concern with more recent outside interventions, but there are no discussions of multinational companies. Trade unions are barely mentioned. Social protests figure only intermittently. Revolutions are quickly passed over unless they can be deemed a "glorious" contribution to progress and productivity.

Can we go beyond this? The International Labour Organization has argued for some time that productivity across the world can and should be based on a "decent work agenda". In the developing countries this needs to be supplemented by "social upgrading" as well as economic upgrading. These arguments have now been formally incorporated into the bigger international development agenda. Unfortunately, they still reflect a top-down approach. The appeal is to mutual self-interest. Social and political gains are "sold" as a means of improving productivity growth and profitability.

A more radical approach is to look for bottom-up growth that could incorporate more equitable and democratic forms of productivity gains. Amartya Sen, for example, argued that the goal of development should be to increase human freedom. We have to aim to increase people's abilities and capabilities and to widen their real choices. This has an economic component, but it cannot be limited to the economic. Freedom should involve being able to live without fear of starvation, undernourishment, illness and premature death, while being literate, numerate and able to speak freely and participate fully in political life. These things should not be seen as by-products of productivity growth: they are ends in themselves.

The question is, can this agenda be developed using existing approaches? Benjamin Selwyn argues that it requires a different, "labour centred development" focus. To be free in Sen's sense means us becoming the "architects of [our] own development" and stopping being the instruments of an endless drive to accumulate, produce more and drive the global economy forwards (Selwyn 2011: 75). We need then to think about the economic and social structures that produce these drives and how we can break with them. Neither market nor statist approaches, which tell us that the only way forward is to accept the world as it is and to knuckle down and be more productive, are adequate (Selwyn 2014). Such discussions take us back to the arguments over whether productivity growth is a means or an end. They also have a very practical significance. If a market-led model cannot develop the whole world, and if there are also limits to replicating any East Asian or Chinese "model", then how do we move forwards? No region raises this question more sharply than sub-Saharan Africa, to which we turn next.

# 7

# Coming last? Low productivity in Africa

Africa, the world's poorest continent, is where productivity remains the low-est. Once largely ignored by the rest of the world, today its problems attract attention from many mainstream economists. A billion people – one-seventh of the world's population – live there. Some are incredibly rich. Some are called middle class, but being "middle class" in Africa is very different from in the advanced world: your income may well be less than the minimum wage in the UK, but enough to have an inside toilet and a generator for when the official electricity fails, as it does on a regular basis (Hammond 2014). Most are poor, although the level of poverty overall has declined (by how much is disputed). Yet Africa is where the first human societies were created. Poverty in Africa, Jared Diamond once wrote, is "the opposite of what one would expect from the runner first off the block" (Diamond 2005).

Our interest here is sub-Saharan Africa. Table 7.1. shows the comparative data for sub-Saharan African productivity levels measured as a percentage of the US level. Looking at individual economies, we see some of the low-est levels of productivity in the world. Productivity *is* advancing, but more slowly than in most of the rest of the world. Table 7.2 shows the result: in relative terms Africa has fallen further behind.

Views of progress in Africa have swung between "Afro-optimism" and "Afro-pessimism". In the 1960s, optimism was in the ascendant. Then, from 1970 to around 2000, pessimism became dominant. In 2000, *The Economist* magazine declared that Africa was "the hopeless continent". Many in Africa were offended, but some who lived there were just as brutal: "Wherever we look", wrote one Nigerian civil rights activist in 1999, "Africa spells failure on all fronts: political, economic, and moral" (Kukah 1999). Growth picked up in the 2000s. This led to talk of "Africa rising" and "African lions" (there are no tigers in Africa), but the surge seemed to falter. The pessimistic view

**Table 7.1** Labour productivity: GDP per employed person 2017 as percentage of US level

|  | Population 2017 (millions) | GDP per person employed as %, US, 2017 |
|---|---|---|
| Sub-Saharan Africa | 1,001 | 8 |
| South Africa | 57 | 35 |
| Nigeria | 191 | 14 |
| Angola | 30 | 14 |
| Ghana | 29 | 8 |
| Kenya | 50 | 7 |
| Tanzania | 55 | 5 |
| Ethiopia | 106 | 3 |
| Mozambique | 29 | 3 |
| Congo (DRC) | 81 | 2 |
| Sudan | 41 | na |

*Source*: US Conference Board.

**Table 7.2** Aggregate labour productivity relative to US (=100), 1960–2014

|  | Industrial economies | Non-sub-Saharan Africa developing countries | Sub-Saharan Africa |
|---|---|---|---|
| 1960 | 53.7 | 17.6 | 6.4 |
| 2014 | 77.8 | 31.7 | 3.2 |

*Source*: *Africa's Pulse* (2018: 68).

is still widespread among economists who focus on the "African growth tragedy" and its "chronic growth failure". This failure has become a stylized fact of economic history. To explain it, people then look for some "character flaw" which is either unique to Africa or, more likely, occurs there in a more concentrated form. But is this stylized fact right?

## The uncertain story of African economic performance

There is no doubt that Africa ranks low in the indicators of absolute productivity levels. But African growth has not always been subpar. Table 7.3 uses the data set created by Angus Maddison to show some long-run trends. Morten Jerven argues that these data do not reflect the historical productivity growth that came from specialization (the types of things talked about by Adam Smith that we looked at in Chapter 2) and the arrival of new crops and techniques (Jerven 2015). He may well be right, but even the Maddison data set shows the problem with the idea that the African past is all much the same. We can see that in one period "Africa" grew faster than the world as a whole. Indeed, if we break down the period 1950–73 at the start of decolonization then this is even true of the 1960s. And when Africa grew less fast than the rest of the world the size of the difference still varied. It was its greatest in the 1980s and 1990s. It is this period which is then read back or averaged into a longer view of Africa's problems.

**Table 7.3** Growth of GDP per head in world and Africa, 1820–2001

|  | World | Africa | Africa's rate as % of world |
|---|---|---|---|
| 1820–70 | 0.54 | 0.35 | 65 |
| 1870–1913 | 1.30 | 0.57 | 44 |
| 1913–50 | 0.88 | 0.92 | 105 |
| 1950–73 | 2.92 | 2.00 | 68 |
| 1973–2001 | 1.41 | 0.19 | 13 |

*Source*: Maddison database.

Table 7.4 shows the most recent data on productivity growth in Africa. Since 2000 "Africa" has grown faster in some years and slower in others, but the growth gap has been nothing like it was at the lowest point. Recent performance is much closer to the world average and for some years above it.

Clearly, we are not looking at South Korean, Chinese or even Indian performance levels, but as Jerven says, "in contrast to what the growth literature tells us, the African growth experience has not been one of persistent

**Table 7.4** Comparative rates of GDP growth per head, 2000–17

|  | 2000–7 | 2008–15 | 2016–17 | GDP per head as %, US |
|---|---|---|---|---|
| US | 2.1 | 1.1 | 1.7 |  |
| World | 3.0 | 1.1 | 0.4 | 100 |
| Latin America | 1.1 | 0.5 | −0.6 | 28 |
| Other developing Asia | 3.5 | 3.0 | 3.8 | 17 |
| Sub-Saharan Africa | 3.2 | 2.1 | −0.9 | 8 |

*Source*: US Conference Board.

**Table 7.5** Sub-Saharan Africa: economic indicators, growth averages per decade

|  | Population (million) | GDP per capita (constant $) | Annual growth (%) | Adult literacy 15+ | Life expectancy | Countries in armed conflict |
|---|---|---|---|---|---|---|
| 1961–70 | 264 | 1,432 | 2.39 | na | 43 | 7.0 |
| 1971–80 | 343 | 1,761 | 0.91 | na | 47 | 8.5 |
| 1981–90 | 454 | 1,651 | −0.95 | 53 | 49 | 11.9 |
| 1991–2000 | 595 | 1,541 | −0.33 | 57 | 49 | 13.1 |
| 2001–10 | 766 | 1,818 | 2.26 | 62 | 52 | 10.3 |

*Source*: Fuglie and Rada (2013: 3).

stagnation" (Jerven 2015: 28). Table 7.5 shows that there have also been social improvements even when economic performance has been less impressive.

Social indicators are important. Africa will soon become more urban than rural; its population is already more literate and educated. People live longer, and infant mortality has declined. All of this undermines both the "stylized fact" and the "character flaw arguments" that are used to explain it. If there is variation you cannot explain it by a constant factor. But how reliable are the data?

## African productivity and damned statistics?

Economists who try to explain economic performance in Africa draw on increasingly extensive global databases and, where these fall short, researchers show great ingenuity in finding proxy data for missing or poorly measured variables. The result, however, is not a happy one. It seems that there is evidence for almost every hypothesis advanced. This is partly because of confirmation bias (people reporting the results that confirm their hypotheses) and partly because of publication bias (the preference – especially in economics – for reporting "positive results" rather than testing and refuting existing ones). Consequently, we have too many explanations for problems in Africa rather than too few. Most of these studies are also examples of the "ingredients" approach that we criticized in Chapter 2. They tell us what ingredients matter, not how to get and use them. The studies also suffer from not being able to adequately distinguish cause and effect. There is clearly an association, for example, between good institutions, good policies (whatever these may be) and good productivity levels, but do good institutions and good policies cause productivity to rise or are they a consequence of successfully increasing productivity in the first place?

We are not even sure we can tell a correct story about the levels of productivity in Africa, their direction of change and their rates of change. "Poor numbers will mislead us", argues Jerven, who has forcefully confronted this problem (Jerven 2013; 2015: 13). The data in the global databases are supplied by national statistical offices which often have to prioritize international agencies rather than their "domestic audiences". Basic population data rely on intermittent censuses with different degrees of accuracy and uncertain processes of the registration of births and deaths. Output data are often weaker. There is a preference for household surveys to measure poverty rather than surveys to enable us to better understand output in agriculture, industry and services, especially in the informal sector. This is particularly disabling for the conventional story which tells us that productivity is the key to relieving poverty.

Putting the data together is also a problem. Much publicity has been given to the way that changing the base year in the calculation of GDP in different African countries has resulted in big changes in their output figures. When Nigeria rebased its GDP figures in 2014, the size of its economy appeared to more or less double. This put Nigeria ahead of South Africa as the biggest economy on the continent and, given that Nigerians make up some 19 per cent of sub-Saharan Africa's population, it had a major impact on any figure for output for "Africa" as a whole.

Jerven has shown that the African data in three of the standard global series of GDP and GDP per head for 30 sub-Saharan African countries do not consistently rank them, let alone agree on smaller differences. Despite the statistics, these countries were "quite similar in terms of income". Big explanations cannot be founded in seemingly small differences in the data.

Can we not find another way of estimating output? One suggestion is that it can be measured indirectly by looking at satellite imagery of light intensity (Pilling 2018a). As output per head rises so more is spent on lighting. The formal electricity output does not measure this because supply is so patchy in poor countries that private generators are common. But images of light intensity are of limited use historically. Nor is it clear how close any light intensity relationship is with output as a whole or output per head. Such calculations do not help us measure inputs either, so measuring productivity change is still a problem. Indeed, light intensity is perhaps the *reductio ad absurdum* of GDP measurement. It uses a "bad" to measure output as a "good". The light seen from space is, after all, waste: it is largely light pollution.

Global databases also contain other problematic data. They use "subjective data" for hard-to-measure things like transparency, corruption and institutional quality. Here there is no objective definition to aspire to. Such softer indices are based on opinion surveys. But the questions of whose opinion, its basis and the problem of perception and misperception are too rarely posed. All of this plays havoc with productivity measurements, and as we dig into Africa's productivity stories we therefore need to keep these problems continually in mind. But detecting any pattern is also difficult due to the huge size and variety of sub-Saharan Africa.

## Variation, volatility and vulnerability

The term "Africa" is a geographical designation. Conventional world maps do not do Africa justice. With over a billion people living across a huge landmass, with a variety of customs, cultures and historical experiences, there can be no African "essence", no "African" explanatory variable. The idea of an "African" character flaw makes no sense once the variation is understood (Ayuba & Haynes 2017).

Today Africa is divided into over 50 nation states. The largest by territory is Algeria, the smallest are the "African islands". On the main land mass Gambia is the smallest with just over 10,000 km² of territory. It has a population of just over 2 million. At the other extreme, Nigeria leads in population terms with perhaps 190 million people (no one knows for sure). These African states are all a product of colonial division. After slavery gave way to what was called "legitimate commerce", Europeans began to penetrate inwards from the coasts. At the end of the nineteenth century the advisers to the leaders of the European states drew most of the lines on the map to create their African empires. These lines bore little relation to what had existed before: look at the number of straight lines on the map. Colonial legacies continue to divide the continent's states and help to mould their cultures, language affiliations, political systems and economies. Since the colonies became independent states what has been remarkable is how small have been the changes to the lines on the maps, how limited the fragmentation. A continent-wide analysis can also be dangerous in other ways. In one study of the period 1970–2015, most African countries advanced (don't forget the data problem). But 29 of 45 countries counted still experienced a relative decline, while only 16 saw a relative improvement. Two – Botswana and Equatorial Guinea – had average annual growth rates in excess of 3.5 per cent (*Africa's Pulse* 2018: 68).

There are many ways to group the economies of Africa in order to explore such variations: geography, levels of development, etc. But one divide commands particular attention. This is the divide between those countries that have valuable raw materials to sell – oil and minerals – and those that do not. We have seen that a lack of natural resources need not preclude development. But what if the problem is the opposite: abundance? This is the idea of "a natural resource curse" (Collier 2007, 2009). Table 7.6 shows those countries in sub-Saharan Africa to which this argument might be most applicable. Africa is estimated to hold 10 per cent of the world's oil reserves, 40 per cent of the gold and 80–90 per cent of metals like chromium and platinum. While some see having natural resources as an opportunity, others argue that it can create dualistic economic structures that depend on global markets.

Volatility is a second problem in understanding African economic performance and its productivity problems. Output figures will always tend to be more volatile if a country relies heavily on agriculture. The harvest will have a greater impact. Volatility will also be greater if a country has a high dependence on foreign trade. Think of the movement in the prices of foodstuffs or oil. The price of oil rose over eight times, from $12 a barrel in 1998 to a peak in 2008; it then dipped, rose again to a new peak in 2012, then fell by 60 per cent to 2016 before rising again. As this happened, the fortunes of

**Table 7.6** Resource curse or opportunity? African resource economies

| Oil | | Metals and minerals | |
|---|---|---|---|
| Angola | Nigeria | Botswana | Mauritania |
| Chad | South Sudan | Congo, DRC | Namibia |
| Congo, DRC | | Guinea | Niger |
| Equatorial Guinea | | Liberia | Sierra Leone |
| Gabon | | | Zambia |

oil economies rose and fell, and so did the illusion of productivity growth as the value of output rose. Such windfall gains encourage internally distorted economies in which parasitic classes and structures feed off "rents" rather than economic improvements that can lead to sustained productivity growth across an economy.

Vulnerability is a third major issue. It arises from the extreme external orientation of sub-Saharan Africa. What Jean-François Bayart called "extraversion" can be seen in everything from political structures to transport infrastructures (Bayart & Ellis 2000). "Extraversion" is something which is externally imposed, directly and indirectly, but it is also something within which African elites have to try to work. "African agency" has always existed but its nature, degree and direction has varied depending on which Africans we are looking at and when. Agency is constrained because external relations are asymmetric. It could be argued that this is true of all economic relations, but the asymmetry in Africa's relations with the big powers is considerable.

Trade openness is an example of this. Jerven suggests that the trade ratio (imports and exports as a share of output) rose from around 10 per cent in the mid-nineteenth century to 40 per cent in 1913 and 50 per cent by the time of independence. It then rose further, fluctuating in relation to global prices, and peaked at around 75 per cent in the 2000s. Most of Africa's trade is conducted by Western multinationals which have traditionally had the upper hand in setting the terms. One American diplomat said that at the time of independence, the new governments "didn't know a thing about the oil business and let the foreign companies define the terms" (French 2005: 74).

Asymmetry is also evident in the external policy regimes that African countries face. In 2002, Joseph Stiglitz wrote that, "the critics of globalization accuse Western countries of hypocrisies and the critics are right. The Western countries have pushed poor countries or eliminated trade barriers but kept up their own barriers ... depriving them of desperately needed export income" (Stiglitz 2002: 6). Nearly two decades on, little has changed. Even ostensible fair-trade products like coffee and chocolate are processed in the advanced world. The growing global intellectual property rights regime also imposes significant costs on poorer countries, such as those in Africa.

The role of exogenous factors is therefore considerable, even though many economists like to focus on "the endogenous". This extends to politics and policy. During the Cold War, Western policy-makers used the carrot and the stick to keep its favoured states on side (the USSR had a more limited capacity to influence events). Big power influence has been exercised by overt and covert means as well as in a semi-detached manner by global institutions. Africa's governments have lacked the room for manoeuvre that the leaders of the East Asian miracle economies were able to exploit. Economists like Paul Collier now argue that economic weakness led to political weakness which in turn has fed back into continued economic weakness. Looking at the period since independence, he noted in 2009 that there had been 82 successful coups in Africa, 109 attempted coups and 145 plots which did not get off the ground (Collier 2009: 8). The question he did not pose is how many of these coups were supported by outside powers, how many were assisted by them and how many were actively provoked by them. "For all their gilded rhetoric about democracy and human rights the actions of the United States, France and Britain had long shown a pronounced preference for the devils they knew well in Africa, Abacha, Mobutu, the apartheid system in South Africa – over the untidiness of their democratic opponents", wrote one close observer (French 2005: 30). Over time external state pressures have then been supplemented by pressures from the IMF, World Bank and later the WTO. In the 1990s many of Africa's leaders "ruled at the pleasure of the so-called international financial institutions ... These almighty international financial institutions had become a virtual government in absentia for the entire African continent in the post-Cold War era" (French 2005: 151, 156).

This is evident in the way that the international institutions used debt crises to impose "structural adjustment programmes". These programmes offered the prospect of a better economic performance if governments privatized and opened up their economies. "Compliance with the prescribed treatment trumped everything else – even the survival of the patient" (French 2005: 158). This produced a situation where any "African failure" can just as easily be seen as an exogenously induced policy as an endogenous one. Such programmes not only undermined economic progress, they also weakened the capacity of states to play a more positive role in the future (Reinsberg et al. 2019).

## Land, labour and capital

We can think about productivity in sub-Saharan Africa in a conventional way. The land input in Africa is limited by physical and climatic conditions. Land

**Table 7.7** Agricultural land and labour inputs in sub-Saharan Africa

|  | Crop area (million ha) | Permanent pasture (million ha) | Labour force (millions) | Area harvested per worker (ha) |
|---|---|---|---|---|
| 1961–70 | 93 | 704 | 81 | 1.15 |
| 1971–80 | 100 | 708 | 96 | 1.04 |
| 1981–90 | 110 | 714 | 118 | 0.93 |
| 1991–2000 | 147 | 731 | 149 | 0.99 |
| 2001–8 | 175 | 746 | 180 | 0.97 |

*Source*: Fuglie and Rada (2013: 6).

can be improved and used more intensively and its use switched between cropping and pasture. Table 7.7 gives estimates of the crude land and labour input to agriculture. We can see that there has been expansion of the land used for farming, although more would be possible. Insofar as this land is being used more intensively this seems to be due as much to the reduction of fallow, as other forms of land improvement are still weak. Furthermore, the United Nations Food and Agriculture Organization (FAO) suspect that the land data are an underestimate. This would then reduce productivity gains in agriculture further. We can also see the increase in the agricultural labour force; the hours input is, however, more uncertain.

Tracking the labour force increase in poor countries is a nightmare because of the scale of unrecorded domestic labour and of underemployed paid labour. With a young population we would expect there to be an increase in the real paid labour input, but for the overall participation rate also to be affected the other way by rising education and increased longevity. If we take the data for sub-Saharan Africa as a whole, then it seems as if employment is growing at around 3 per cent per year. Unfortunately, output growth has fluctuated around a lower trend so it looks as if output per worker is declining. This suggests the urbanization and the shift to the informal economy involves a shift from underemployed rural labour to underemployed urban labour. The productivity of underemployed urban labour may still be higher than that of underemployed rural labour, but this situation is far from positive. More positive is the improvement in labour force quality seen in rising education levels. Although Africa's educational catch-up is still lagging behind, it is still impressive, as Tables 7.8 and 7.9 show.

In sub-Saharan Africa the accumulation of physical capital is weak and the capital intensity of output the lowest in the world. The gap in some areas

**Table 7.8** Percentage primary school enrolment, 1820–2010

|      | High income | Europe & Central Asia | Latin America & Caribbean | Middle East & North Africa | East Asia | South Asia | Sub-Saharan Africa |
|------|-------------|----------------------|---------------------------|----------------------------|-----------|------------|--------------------|
| 1820 | 19.72       | 2.94                 | 1.79                      | 0.09                       | 0.00      | 0.09       | 0.22               |
| 1850 | 36.26       | 4.66                 | 5.78                      | 0.33                       | 0.03      | 0.37       | 0.85               |
| 1900 | 74.38       | 33.33                | 21.65                     | 3.62                       | 2.10      | 6.40       | 2.83               |
| 1950 | 95.43       | 85.66                | 49.25                     | 28.61                      | 37.52     | 31.54      | 29.86              |
| 1960 | 94.65       | 82.46                | 66.53                     | 43.52                      | 67.85     | 44.23      | 48.60              |
| 1980 | 95.80       | 91.55                | 84.45                     | 77.89                      | 82.17     | 59.38      | 58.75              |
| 2000 | 99.54       | 98.63                | 98.78                     | 89.51                      | 99.53     | 87.93      | 72.07              |
| 2010 | 99.34       | 99.05                | 99.47                     | 98.00                      | 99.58     | 97.54      | 90.05              |

*Source*: Lee and Lee (2016) dataset.

has reduced but not agriculture. The FAO estimates that while the agricultural capital stocks grew in sub-Saharan Africa at around 1.5 per cent per year for the mid-1970s to the mid-2000s, the labour force grew at 2 per cent, resulting in a −0.5 per cent growth in capital stock per worker. Table 7.10 shows some of the components here. The biggest source of output increase has come from the use of new varieties, but even here the percentage of cropland sown with them remains small. Livestock herds have grown too. Other indicators are more negative and (allowing for measurement problems) a sign of the continued neglect of agriculture.

**Table 7.9** Percentage secondary school enrolment, 1820–2010

|      | High income | Europe & Central Asia | Latin America & Caribbean | Middle East & North Africa | East Asia | South Asia | Sub-Saharan Africa |
|------|-------------|----------------------|---------------------------|----------------------------|-----------|------------|--------------------|
| 1820 | 0.26        | 0.13                 | 0.01                      | 0.00                       | 0.00      | 0.03       | 0.00               |
| 1850 | 1.39        | 0.15                 | 0.03                      | 0.01                       | 0.00      | 0.13       | 0.00               |
| 1900 | 5.32        | 1.58                 | 0.44                      | 0.15                       | 0.05      | 1.01       | 0.02               |
| 1950 | 26.84       | 13.12                | 3.19                      | 5.54                       | 1.90      | 8.25       | 1.84               |
| 1960 | 52.74       | 42.90                | 8.71                      | 9.27                       | 17.89     | 13.99      | 3.50               |
| 1980 | 75.51       | 73.00                | 28.06                     | 34.15                      | 39.79     | 22.25      | 15.85              |
| 2000 | 91.94       | 83.67                | 72.55                     | 57.88                      | 57.32     | 42.02      | 29.56              |
| 2010 | 93.62       | 85.02                | 81.88                     | 66.82                      | 80.60     | 57.11      | 41.94              |

*Source*: Lee and Lee (2016) dataset.

**Table 7.10** Some components of the capital intensity of agriculture in sub-Saharan Africa

|  | Tractors per 1,000 hectares | Area harvested irrigated (%) | Crop area using improved varieties (%) | Fertiliser (kg per hectare) | Livestock (cattle equivalent, million) |
|---|---|---|---|---|---|
| 1961–70 | 0.69 | 3.09 | 0.5 | 3.04 | 172 |
| 1971–80 | 0.94 | 3.46 | 0.2 | 7.07 | 206 |
| 1981–90 | 0.99 | 3.90 | 8.6 | 9.95 | 241 |
| 1991–2000 | 0.86 | 3.51 | 14.9 | 8.57 | 283 |
| 2001–8 | 0.87 | 3.22 | 21.0 | 7.62 | 352 |

*Source*: Fuglie and Rada 2013: 6.

The World Bank has been monitoring the quantity, quality and ease of access to Africa's infrastructure, and here too the picture remains poor. The mobile phone revolution has seen the numbers with access to a phone rise from 3 per 1,000 in 1990 to some 800 plus per 1,000 today. This is an astonishing turnaround which has been widely seen to prefigure a possible leapfrogging forwards not only in human relations but information supply and even finance through phone apps like M-Pesa. Sadly, it tells us nothing about the wider infrastructure. The electricity to charge these phones is a problem (it is often sold by small businesses sometimes using solar power, sometimes generators). Two-thirds of the population still lack access to an electricity supply and that which exists often goes down. When it does not, most of it goes to supply offices, factories and the homes of the wealthy. On some accounts the road and rail density has actually worsened over the last three decades. Access to clean water and sanitation has improved but is still a huge problem. Africa today (like India too) has many times more mobile phones than toilets. It is easy to see, then, why even someone like Bill Gates should be so sceptical of the idea of an internet-savvy Africa finding a techno fix: "I certainly don't think giving everyone computers helps their malaria or solves the problem of the teacher not being there or not having a schoolroom" (quoted in Pilling 2018b).

## African productivity growth and structural change

Structural change and productivity growth exists in Africa too, but the pattern is different from that in South Korea and China (less so India), and even more different from those of the early industrializers. People are moving more from agriculture to services and often to lower-productivity services activity rather than into manufacturing. If we take the decade 2000–10, for example, only 20 per cent of those who left agriculture went into manufacturing in its widest sense: 80 per cent went into the service sector. And here, "a majority of jobs are being provided by the traditional services industries across the African continent" (Enache *et al.* 2016: 16). The largest part of the service sector in Africa is trade and much of it remains small-scale trading. Table 7.11 shows us the basic pattern over the last 60 years.

**Table 7.11** The peculiar pattern of growth and structural change in sub-Saharan Africa, 1960–2010

|  | Population (millions) | Index GDP per head | Urban (%) | Employment shares | | | Value added shares current prices | | |
|---|---|---|---|---|---|---|---|---|---|
|  |  |  |  | Ag. | Indus. | Ser. | Ag. | Indus. | Ser. |
| 1960 | 221 | 100 | 14.9 | 73 | 9 | 18 | 38 | 24 | 38 |
| 1975 | 324 | 109 | 20.4 | 66 | 13 | 21 | 29 | 30 | 41 |
| 1990 | 493 | 114 | 27.5 | 62 | 14 | 24 | 25 | 33 | 43 |
| 2010 | 845 | 139 | 36.1 | 51 | 13 | 37 | 22 | 28 | 50 |

*Source*: Groningen (GGDC) ten-sector and related databases.

We can see that although the growth of employment in the industry sector was not spectacular from the 1960s to the 1980s, the pattern has some similarity to that which we have analysed elsewhere. But even then doubts were being expressed about the extent to which an agricultural–manufacturing shift was boosting productivity. Since then there has only been limited evidence of the growth in the share of manufacturing employment. It is the service sector that surges.

Table 7.11 also points to the contrast between the labour force share and the value-added share. In 1960 a service worker was roughly twice as productive as an agricultural worker and a worker in industry 2.6 times as productive. By 2010 value added per worker in industry was some five times

147

that of a worker in agriculture. Value added in the service sector was some three times higher.

What of a techno fix through "leapfrog technologies". This is the argument we noted for India now applied to Africa. The hope is that Africa might find new competitive niches and jump forwards in ways not possible in the past. Some have tried to relate new technologies to different types of production and activity in which Africa might have an advantage. Could productivity growth in Africa be based on "industries without smokestacks", such as horticulture, tourism and high-end services (Newfarmer *et al.* 2019)? Flowers, grown on a large scale by horticulturalists in Africa, now arrive in Europe. Tourism is significant for some countries. But even if we ignore the complications that these types of activities also bring, it seems fanciful to imagine that the productivity problems of a billion people can be solved by turning one part of the continent into a giant market garden, another part into a giant safari park and a third into a financial hub. These sectors look to have high value-added as much because of the low valued-added elsewhere as their intrinsic merits. They may not be the enclaves that some sectors have been in the past, but their development does not maximize linkages to the rest of the economy. Tourism, for example, may need a smart app, a good road to the smart hotel, shopping mall and safari park, but this does not automatically feed through into the building of wider road systems, electricity grids or the other infrastructures that Africa desperately needs.

## The formal and informal sectors

Africa is not without some large-scale, high-productivity production. Colonialism established a division between peasant and large-scale farming depending on the country and type of food products that still operates today. Horticultural production has developed with the large-scale production of flowers and some vegetables which end up in Western supermarkets. In raw material extraction, the oil industry is obviously high technology. Other raw materials like coltan – vital for computers – are won by alluvial mining amid economic and political repression, violence and warfare. In the manufacturing and services sector multinationals have set up operations with high levels of capital investment and productivity. Many of their operations tend to be focused on the consumer market. Companies like Proctor and Gamble, Unilever and Coca Cola have long histories in Africa. Some local successes have been bought out. Walmart took a controlling share of Massmart, which in 2018 operated over 400 stores in 12 countries. South Africa has a more advanced economy and it is the base of some of the biggest sub-Saharan-owned companies, like MTN (mobile), Bidvest (services), Eskom (power) and Shoprite (retail) which reach out across the continent. In West Africa, Dangote Industries is a huge conglomerate. Belying cultural stereotypes, its founder, Aliko Dangote, grew up as a Hausa Muslim from Kano state in Nigeria's north. Today, Dangote is said to be the richest person on the subcontinent. Dangote Industries developed out of trade and food processing, where it produced and packaged flour, rice, pasta, sugar and soft drinks, and moved into building materials like cement. It is now extending into fibre optics and beyond (Akinyoade & Uche 2016). There is even a Nigerian motor manufacturer, and more importantly a Nollywood film production sector. But in terms of employment these modern enterprises employ relatively few people. Dangote, for example, has only 11,000 employees.

The scale of the growth of the informal sector is puzzling. Most Africans in the burgeoning cities survive by working for themselves or in small-scale enterprises on the border of legality. Some see informality as a reservoir of opportunities for entrepreneurial talent. Aliko Dangote is supposed to have said that, "when I was in primary school, I would go and buy cartons of sweets and I would start selling them just to make money. I was so interested in business, even at that time." But rags to riches stories are rare and often much less simple than they seem. Others see informality as a manifestation of degeneration in the growth process. There is little doubt that the majority of people in the informal sector are there because they have no other way of making a living. Their story is about survival.

Measuring the size of the informal sector, whether in terms of its labour force or output, is fraught with difficulties. But the broad outlines seem clear enough. Informality in Africa may be at more or less similar levels to Latin America, but it is higher than South Asia and much higher that in the most advanced economies. Overall the share of output coming from the informal sector may be around 40 per cent, with a higher share in the least developed economies. Those economies with a high natural resource dependence seem to have the highest informal share of all, not least an economy like Nigeria's. One recent study of 37 of Africa's 50 plus countries suggested that in eight the share of the informal sector in output was between 20 and 30 per cent. It was between 30 and 40 per cent in 17 and between 40 and 50 per cent in ten. It was over 50 per cent in Tanzania and over 60 per cent in Nigeria, Africa's largest economy (Medina *et al.* 2016: 30).

Survival labour in the informal sector is conventionally thought to be less productive than it is for those whose efforts are motivated by opportunity: think the ubiquitous underemployed roadside food sellers. But measurement is almost impossible. How big are the inputs and outputs and how do we value them? Just because the informal sector exists on the margins, often beyond the sphere of regulation and taxation, the fact that people earn incomes there does not necessarily mean that they are adding value to society. Baumol's distinction between entrepreneurship that is productive, unproductive and destructive is again helpful. In the informal economy we find each kind of activity, but it could be argued that much of the effort there is about gains from unproductive and destructive activities. These add nothing to and perhaps subtract from productivity overall. In practice an activity may combine several elements, as when a counterfeit producer "creates value by producing" but "steals value" by fraudulently copying the design and perhaps destroys it by "bribing the local authorities" to turn a blind eye. The simple argument that a way must be found to formalize the informal sector collapses if it can only survive because of its informality. But the opposite argument that rules are made to be broken also seems unhelpful if they lead to perverse forms of growth.

It is sometimes argued that ultimately wages will rise in other parts of the world, making cheap labour in Africa more attractive and therefore eventually attracting more production from the formal sector. This seems unlikely. Competition from other parts of the global economy now severely limits the development space in Africa. The textile industry has often been a first step towards economic upgrading. The number of workers in the global textile industry has risen to some 60–75 million workers but they are concentrated in a few countries. The same applies to shoes. There is little "economic space" for Africa to use the textile industry as a stepping stone to higher productivity. The least developed countries trying to get in on this sector face "a rocky road ahead" according to the International Labour Organization (ILO 2019). Their problems are compounded by the way in which the rich world passes on some 4 million tons of used clothing each year. Most gets sold in poor countries: 70 per cent of the world's population is said to wear second-hand clothes. African producers, therefore, face a double whammy of competition from the big clothing exporters and from the second-hand importers. It is hardly surprising that textile employment in some countries has fallen. Ever optimistic, the African Development Bank has argued that high-end fashion exports might create 400,000 jobs by 2025 and an additional $2 billion of exports. But this is a drop in the ocean. It would still be less than 1 per cent of the global textile and clothing trade. High productivity though this niche might be, the washing, repairing and selling of second-hand clothes in the informal sector is likely to be more significant for many in Africa, even if it does compromise the role of formal clothing production.

## Debating the deeper causes of low productivity in Africa

The other side of the attempt to find deeper causes of the success of the East Asian economies is the search for the root causes of "African failure". Some argue that Africa has suffered from a negative path dependency, locked in by difficult initial conditions. These are not new arguments but they can take on modern guises. Jeffrey Sachs argues that sub-Saharan Africa suffers from geographical and climatic constraints. Forty per cent of people, for example, live in landlocked countries. Africa's impressive rivers are not eas- ily navigable, nor are its coasts such that ports are easy to construct. Climate, too, encourages endemic diseases which debilitate those who have them and have kept the death rate high. Others see path dependency in rather different ways. Despite a growing population, some argue that Africa in the past has had a low ratio of people to land. This has made labour costs high and deterred progress (Austin 2008). There is some irony in this argument because, as we have seen, in other cases higher historical productivity growth has been argued to have been a response to high labour costs (Allen 2011).

Initial conditions easily slide over into the discussion of institutions. Acemoglu and Robinson, whose institutional account we noticed in Chapter 6, argue that people in Africa have continually shown a capacity for economic advance, but they have been derailed by the imposition of extractive institu- tional regimes from slavery and colonialism onwards. It is these structures which have undermined productivity-enhancing "creative destruction and technological change". They tend to eschew the word capitalism but, in their account, they argue that European colonization re-enforced or created coercive institutions in Africa which survived decolonization. A more positive form of capitalism in one part of the world created a more negative form in another. This part of their account overlaps considerably with more radical ones. The implication is clear: it could have been different, and the solution in the future lies within Africa in terms of the restructuring of economic and political institutions to make them more inclusive and productivity inducing. What they are less clear about is how these changes are to be made.

Their reluctance is not shared by those in the international institutions, who continue to focus on improved markets and market institutions as the high road to productivity growth. Studies of IMF conditionality, for example, have shown little detailed change in the prescriptions despite a rhetoric to the contrary (Kentikelenis *et al.* 2016). The World Bank now claims that:

> the lower labour productivity in sub-Saharan Africa is explained by inefficiencies in the allocation of resources across firms and farms ... misallocation (inefficiencies in the use of technologies) has become relatively more important than undercapitalization (low capital stock) in driving these productivity differences.
>
> (*Africa's Pulse* 2018: 2)

Misallocation is part of the productivity problem but it cannot be detached from undercapitalization.

To do so leads to distorted measures of success. In the 1960s and 1970s, Western institutions needed positive examples of success, so they worked with local leaders to create what were called in French *vitrines du capitalism*: showcases of capitalism. These showcases were real things: factories, dams, roads, urban developments. In the 1980s and 1990s the showcases became more abstract, associated with high scores for having the right policies. Then a fashion developed for small-scale experimental showcases that demonstrated that things could work with the right incentives. Today these showcases are supplemented by abstract market ones. A functioning stock market or market in land becomes a new showcase of the way forward.

The contrasting approaches to analysing Africa's deeper productivity problems come together in the discussion of capital flight. Africa is an exporter of capital and a large one in relation to its levels of income. Some of this is debt repayment, some of it is legal profit repatriation, but much of it exists in the grey and dark areas of capital movement. If, as we have argued, the most important forms of productivity change have to be embodied in new equipment, buildings and infrastructure then capital flight matters. Capital that could have been invested in Africa is either being spent or deposited in the rich world. This holds down investment. It reduces tax revenues through "base erosion". It contributes to economic and social inequality. This much most commentators agree on. So how much is capital flight an internal or an external problem?

Popular attention tends to be given to the internal kleptocratic elites and Africa's history of dictators who have milked the system for their own ends. We pointed out earlier, however, that Africa's worst rulers historically have had considerable political backing from the US and Europe. And their economic milking of the system could not have occurred without the complicity of the Western banks and high-end salesmen who accepted their money. Before his early death in the 1990s, the Congolese writer Sony Lab'ou Tansi said: "Our leaders follow the examples they were taught by the Europeans, stealing money and never doing anything for the people. I'm calling my newest work 'La Cosa Nostra,' because it's about Africa's dictators and their protectors in Europe" (French 2005: 86).

But what is too often missed is that this debilitating personalized corruption probably amounts to less than 5 per cent of the capital flight that sucks wealth out of Africa. Defining illicit flows is a problem, but a huge part arises because of the activities of Western multinationals which transfer their profits out of Africa under the radar. They do this in two related ways. The first is trade mis-invoicing to avoid border taxes. The second is the transfer pricing we noted in Chapter 3. In this way companies move value across borders between their subsidiaries using internal accounting tricks which set the prices of goods and services below or above their values, so that income in one part of the internal value chain is reduced while it is increased in another.

This is possible partly because of the internal weakness of states and the nature of multinational companies, but also because the wider institutions of the global economy make this a relatively easy thing to do. Indeed, the deregulation of capital movements has even weakened basic checks on the credibility of documentation. And, as with the receipt of corrupt personal money, so too company-based capital flight is only possible because the receiving states and their institutions turn a blind eye to the origins of these flows. Some of these receiving countries are the world's many offshore tax havens, but much of the money ends up in company and bank accounts held "onshore", not least in the UK and the City of London in particular. Such illicit capital flows are by no means unique to Africa, but its lowly position in the global hierarchy means that their productivity-limiting impact there is probably the greatest. One recent UN estimate suggests that between 1970 and 2010 illicit flows out of sub-Saharan Africa were 45 per cent more than total foreign direct investment to Africa and almost three times more than total foreign aid (Ndikumana 2017).

## A Chinese way in Africa?

However attractive the Soviet model might have been at one stage, the USSR itself played a limited role in offering carrots to African regimes to emulate it. The West was always a much bigger source of aid, advice and influence. When the USSR collapsed, the dominance of the West grew even more. But today an alternative pole of attraction exists in the form of China. Its rise to influence in Africa began before the 2008 economic crisis but it has intensified since then. Most focus has been given to China's role in big infrastructure projects – ports, railways and roads – but it is also playing a part in projects linked to manufacturing, agriculture and, less commonly, some services activities. Can China be more successful in assisting Africa to realize a productivity revolution?

Both the West and China say they wish to encourage growth in Africa. The differences between them are over tactics. Their arguments replicate the debate over how China has grown, and the clash between which policies might maximize short-term productivity growth and those that might lead to longer-term productivity growth. One sympathetic commentator said:

> China's own economic development in the past four decades was achieved through making massive State-led investments in infrastructure projects that are often unprofitable. If one only applies a narrowly defined cost-benefit analysis, many of these [...] projects themselves may not be justifiable.
>
> (Gu Qingyang quoted in Xiaodong 2019: 18)

The evaluation of China's current economic influence in Africa is bound up with geopolitics. To the US and its supporters, China appears as a new imperial power seeking to exploit Africa in the same way that other imperial powers have done. China, said Mike Pompeo, when US vice president in 2019, is selling "corrupt infrastructure deals in exchange for political influence" and creating "bribe fuelled debt-trap diplomacy" (quoted in Xiaodong 2019: 17). Let us suspend thoughts about hypocrisy and leave aside too the question of whether both sides see "Africa" primarily in terms of their own needs. The point is that this new competition between the existing big powers and a rising China gives African elites more flexibility when they look for outside help. They can now try to manoeuvre between those trying to influence them.

But it is important to say that China has far from disavowed conventional economic approaches. It has even shown a willingness to work with the IMF and World Bank. At a more detailed level the assessments made by those closely linked to the IMF and World Bank are more positive than might be imagined (Dollar 2018). There is even a claim that Chinese projects, by not focusing on investing in the areas where productivity and profit is already higher, are acting to reduce inequality. A sceptic might argue that these detailed accounts are positive not only because they are less influenced by geopolitical rhetoric but also because they share similar criteria for the evaluation of what works and what does not work. To the extent therefore that China is acting like any other great power, its activities, evaluated by the same logic, will be hard – for good or ill – to separate out.

The bigger problem is whether this is the way forward at all? First, China may be a supporter of change in Africa but it is also a competitor for markets and resources. Take oil. Only 11 per cent of West African oil exports goes to other African states, 33 per cent goes to China, 29 per cent to Europe and 12 and 9 per cent to India and the US, respectively. Africa's proven oil reserves are slightly smaller than its current 10 per cent production share and will be increasingly hard to extract. But if Africa were suddenly to "take off" in the way that China has done (and others did before it) it would need a huge increase in energy output which would undermine its ability to export. If Africa were as successful in the next four decades as China has been in the last four then its energy per capita consumption might have to increase by as much as 15 times.

This feeds into the second problem: the impact that the negative side of any African productivity surge (along with growth elsewhere) might bring.

China is promoting its green credentials in Africa. It says it is focused on environmental concerns, building sustainable foundations, green energy and green technology. It claims to be protecting both people and ecologies. Many accounts dispute this, not least those from inside Africa which have looked carefully at major projects. But even if this is true the bigger question is, would it be enough? Fantasy technologies aside, how is this compatible with dealing with existing environmental problems and global warming?

The third problem is that while the Chinese approach may offer more prospects of success, it still remains very much a top-down approach. Indeed, one of the controversial questions is how much of genuine "African" participation there is in its projects, let alone discussion of their wider wisdom and how they might fit into a sustainable vision of the future? If Chinese workers, for example, have to pay a "China price" for success there, do African workers have to pay an "African price" for progress in their continent too?

We arrive once again at the question of whether any approach based around past productivity growth models can produce future routes to high productivity that are globally sustainable and desirable. As in the rich world, where the focus on the possibilities of productivity growth is used to deflect attention away from the discussions about purpose and redistribution, so the possibilities of productivity growth for the poor world are used to deflect attention from redistribution as a part of the solution to global gaps between the countries. If it is impossible to imagine a situation in which poor countries could ever obtain a level of per capita income of the advanced world, within the limits of what the planet can sustain, then we *do* need to think both about how we can go beyond the conventional approaches to productivity and about redistribution, both *within* economies and *between* them.

# 8

# Productivity in a different world

Our productivity journey has allowed us to see the benefits of productivity growth. We have also seen the complications of its measurement. We have looked at the debates over the causes of productivity growth and the extent to which productivity has a dark side. In Chapter 4 we argued that the past cannot be a guide to the future. Now, having explored some of the variety of actual productivity experiences, we can also see more clearly why we need to think beyond the conventional views of productivity growth as the solution to global problems.

This was the point that Tawney, whom we quoted in Chapter 1, made a century ago. Productivity is a means, not an end, and it is a means that can also be part of the problem that it is said to cure. Tawney was not alone in thinking this. In a 1930 essay, the economist John Maynard Keynes talked about what he called "the economic possibilities for our grandchildren". He was confident that the productivity successes to come would release them from the need to look for never-ending productivity growth. Already by 1930 he had problems with those who wanted to argue that "jam is not jam unless it is a case of jam tomorrow and never jam to-day". This argument would look even more foolish in "a hundred years [when] the economic problem would be solved". In this future world we would have so much that we would need to use fewer inputs, not least our labour. "Three-hour shifts or a fifteen-hour week ... three hours a day is quite enough to satisfy the old Adam in most of us!" (Keynes 1931 [1930]: 370). In a new world of leisure, we would have the opportunity to do many different things. Today we are the grandchildren that Keynes wrote about. Some people reading this book will be the great grandchildren, perhaps the great, great grandchildren of those alive in 1930. Keynes was right. We *have* achieved the miraculous levels of wealth in the rich world that he thought would release us from need and the focus on ever more material wealth. But his predictions of a 15-hour week have not come true: the argument is still that we need to put off having more jam today in order to get more tomorrow. Keynes did not overstate the possibilities of productivity growth; he underestimated the resistance to sharing the gains it has brought. To the extent that this is a problem of ideas – and clearly it is only partly this – we need to do more than think about how we can continue to get *more with less*. We have to look for a "productivity" that more equitably shares what we have and globally delivers us *less with even less*.

## Perverse productivity and mismeasurement

Sometimes an author's mind can wander. Since productivity measures the relationship between outputs and inputs, I have occasionally asked myself what is the most perverse productivity calculation I can imagine? Could we find higher-productivity forms of drug dealing? Maybe we need more accidents to boost measured output and more hot bedding might improve measured hospital productivity. We could increase transport productivity by making the trains even more overcrowded. Maybe we should put more effort into raising the productivity of weapons systems; but they are working on that. Getting "more bang for your buck" is, after all, a productivity concept.

There is a serious point here. We are seeing a more sustained engagement with the limitations and contradictions of GDP as a measure of output. This needs to be extended to the notion of productivity too. This is not simply because, at the level of economies, it uses GDP and its components as its output measure, but because of the logical and practical problems of capturing inputs and processes. Table 8.1 draws together some of the anomalies that undermine the conventional approach to productivity.

Those familiar with the nitty-gritty of the detailed calculations will say that not everything that goes on in the first column is always counted as a good and not everything that goes on in the second column is always ignored. This is true. But this is largely what does happen, and when it does not it is not because the elements are consistently included and properly measured, but because they are arbitrarily identified and often poorly measured. We have asked why, if a value is imputed for one thing it is not done for another? Why not impute the estimated value for sex within relationships?

**Table 8.1** Examples of perverse elements in measured productivity

| Things which appear to improve measured productivity | Things which appear to decrease measured productivity |
|---|---|
| **Outputs** | **Outputs** |
| Climate change | Environmental protection |
| War | Peace |
| Conventional economics | Heterodox economics |
| Pay walls, patents, copyright | Free knowledge |
| Hate | Love and care |
| Prostitution | Free sex |
| Buying and selling | Sharing |
| New stuff | Home production and recycling |
| Inequality | Equality |
| Ill health | Public health and prevention |
| Traffic jams | Cycling, walking, public transport |
| Divorce | Stable relationships |
| | |
| **Processes** | **Processes** |
| Shift working | Doing stuff slowly |
| Rushing | Non-price quality |
| Asset sweating | |
| Short staffing | |
| Hot bedding | |
| "Shrinkflation" | |
| | |
| **Inputs** | **Inputs** |
| Robots | Leisure |
| Unpaid overtime | |
| Skimping | |
| Self-service | |

The craziness lies not in the suggestion but the arbitrary inclusion of one thing and the exclusion of another. What about the inputs and outputs of cycling? Is this trivializing? Not if you live in the Netherlands. Or what of walking in poor countries? What about street begging? Not an output or an input? Give the beggar a tin whistle and you have a street entertainer. Even without the tin whistle, if giving money increases my self-satisfaction then conventional economic logic suggests that because it has value to me it has value to society too. Then necessarily too the hours of the mute labour of the homeless person and the capital investment in a hat or cup to hold my spare change must be an input. We can add the productivity of begging to the perverse thoughts that arise when productivity ends are ignored.

Economic thinking on productivity and its growth needs to be rethought, not as a narrow private sum, but as a calculation which is properly social and therefore more complete:

*NOT*

$$\frac{\text{Increase in private gain}}{\text{Increase in private input}}$$

*BUT*

$$\frac{(\text{Private} + \text{social gain}) - (\text{Private} + \text{social loss})}{\text{Increase in private} + \text{social input}}$$

However difficult this second calculation might be to make, it is essential to any understanding of the real process of productivity growth and to an understanding of both its possibilities and its limits.

Figure 8.1 shows one way of thinking about this drawn from the environmental economist Herman Daly (2005). Using the concepts of "traditional" economics, Daly argues that over time the marginal utility of productivity growth declines due to diminishing returns while its marginal disutility rises. At some point the disutility and utility curves cross and the costs of productivity growth come to outweigh the gains.

The actual balance is an empirical issue. Daly's diagram merely illustrates the need to think this problem through, but he adds a further element. Both

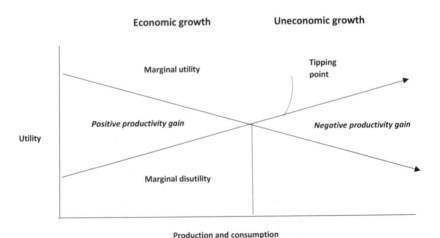

**Figure 8.1** Herman Daly's vision of utility and disutility in growth

curves are drawn as straight lines. The fear, as we saw in Chapter 4, is that when it comes to environmental problems there may well be tipping points where the disutility of productivity growth surges: put more simply, the tipping point in the diagram represents the shift from environmental problems to "crisis", even "catastrophe". Note that Daly draws the tipping point after the utility and disutility curves have crossed. We might want to consider that on some indicators of disutility this crossing point has already been reached. But even if this is not the case, a tipping point could still occur further to the left, before the two curves cross. If we are to avoid this, we need to think about how we can get off the productivity treadmill in the advanced countries and then globally.

## Staying on or getting off the productivity treadmill

When Keynes speculated that higher productivity would enable us to reduce our labour, he thought that people would have a "leisure preference" and reject the attraction of ever more consumption. So, what is it that seems to make us want more productivity in order to get more material goods: more goods whose value is inflated by branding, and more intangible goods whose values are protected by intellectual property rights? Stand outside the logic of modern capitalism and this "preference" seems irrational. Stand inside the system and contesting this logic is still considered subversive. What drives this logic is the combination of three things: consumerism, inequality and the lack of social control over society's priorities.

In Chapter 4 we used the example of cars to see what happens if we project forwards a picture of the future in terms of the past. The trouble is that the same problems emerge wherever we look. Take flying. It is true that the global rich fly most of all but flying rises with incomes. Most of the people alive today in the world have not flown and will never fly. In Africa the number of annual flights per head is only around 0.1. It is 0.25 in Asia and 0.3 in Latin America. Yet in Europe it is just over 1 and in North America it is 2.3. Given how much $CO_2$ an average flight produces, can this go on?

In the rich world we are already drowning in stuff. British consumers buy more clothes per head than any other population in Europe. Yet few of these fast fashion clothes are ever worn for very long, if at all. We are said to have around £10 billion of largely unwanted clothing in our wardrobes and drawers. It is not just clothes. Garages in the advanced world are often so full there is no room for the car(s). But garages are not enough. Today the UK has some 1,500 big box storage units with 45 million square feet of storage space. On top of this the average UK household is said to throw away a ton of "waste" a year, and at the recent rate of increase will double the weight of household waste every 20–25 years. This is certainly a problem of "sustainability", but it is also a problem of rationality of the productivity treadmill that is driven by consumerism.

Much of the stuff we buy – irrespective of the prices we pay – is actually produced by the same people in the same factories. A succession of consumer tests has shown that higher prices and branding is no guarantee of higher quality even if wearing stuff with the right "label" makes us feel good. Today, for many items it is hard to distinguish genuine quality from must have "brand" rents.

Contrary to what economists continue to claim, total demand is *not* unlimited nor is the form that it takes given. Demand is constructed. We do not "need" more cars, for example, we "need" better forms of public transport and a different distribution of work and leisure. This would change the productivity calculation and the balance between total productivity gains and losses. It would require a systematic rethink, but there is no reason why this is not possible.

Inequality is a second related cause of the productivity treadmill. We have seen that economists often see productivity growth as a substitute for equality. If productivity can keep average incomes rising then who cares about redistribution? The perverse consequence of this reasoning has been that the distribution of productivity gains in recent decades has become even more unequal. This makes the idea of an average income even less realistic. It does nothing to deal with the problem of relative poverty. The more unequal the society, the more this feeds into consumerism. Nothing is ever enough, not least at the top where we are existing to admire the lifestyles of the super-elites. The negative material and mental feedback loops that all this produces are well documented and need to be part of any genuine societal productivity calculation.

Consumerism and inequality reflect a third element that sustains the productivity treadmill. This is the lack of social control over the economy. The drive for productivity flows from the way that national economies compete. It flows from the way that businesses compete and it flows from the way that institutions compete. The problem here is not that such competition encourages the privatization of productivity goods and the socialization of productivity bads, although that is certainly important. It is that this competition does not allow us to collectively decide to what ends we wish to put our existing high levels of productivity and their further development. Instead of the economic system being an instrument for us, we become the instruments of the economic system. It is the end and we are the means. Recognizing the extent to which the drive for increased productivity is imposed on us as a race that will never finish is essential if we are to realize the possibilities we already have, let alone those of any worthwhile future.

## A different kind of productivity growth?

In Chapters 4 and 5 we looked at the slowdown of productivity advance at the productivity frontier in the advanced countries. We saw that one view was that the slowdown was an illusion, another was that it was not and that efforts needed to be made to pull productivity growth back to its historical trend level. Both views assume that continued productivity growth is the solution rather a problem. Yet outside of this narrower productivity debate, the temperature of the argument is rising because global temperatures themselves are increasing, making carrying on as before more unrealistic still.

One answer to this is that we should be searching for new forms of green productivity growth and the green new deal we noted in Chapter 4. In his inaugural address, Roosevelt in the 1930s sought to inspire people with a new purpose as part of the first New Deal. "The money changers have fled from their high seats in the temple of our civilisation. We may now restore that temple to the ancient truths. The measure of the restoration lies in the extent to which we apply social values more noble than monetary profit." The idea of a green new deal now finds more mainstream support from economists like Paul Krugman and Joseph Stiglitz, as well as left-of-centre political forces. But would it be enough to subordinate "monetary profit" to social and green values today with a different kind of productivity to that traditionally espoused by economists?

Change has to start somewhere, so such proposals need a sympathetic evaluation, although we should note that they rest on a mythologized historical model. The original New Deal of the 1930s was improvised, limited and inconsistent. It met with huge opposition. What consolidated many of its policies was struggle from below to broaden rights and then the outbreak of war in 1941. For a generation this directly and indirectly changed the way that people thought about the economic system. Today the forces of opposition are just as great. It is not simply that some believe that there is no real problem – it is more the vested interests that might prevent the scale of the rethink that is necessary. President Trump expressed this problem well when he ironically tweeted in February 2019 that "It would be great for the so-called 'Carbon Footprint' to permanently eliminate all Planes, Cars, Cows, Oil, Gas & the military – even if no other country would do the same. Brilliant!"

Sometimes even a tweet from Donald Trump can capture a real problem. A green new deal is a national gesture, not a global one. Given the extent to which the high productivity of the advanced world directly and indirectly uses up global resources and contributes to global warming it is important that national measures are taken, but the competitive nature of the global interstate system makes their generalization hard. Note too how Trump implicitly celebrates the major industrial and commercial interests that have thrived on forms of perverse productivity and perverse productivity accounting.

But there is an even bigger problem. Such green productivity growth does not seem to be enough to deal with the larger environmental issues. It certainly will not be enough if "good green productivity growth" in one area is seen as allowing the continuation of "dirty productivity growth" in another. This has led to new arguments about an improved productivity subordinated to a broader degrowth agenda. Productivity in the future has to be about getting less from even less and not more from less. Degrowth ideas are discussed elsewhere (Kallis 2018). Suffice it to say here that while green productivity growth finds support from economists like Krugman and Stiglitz, they are far less enamoured with degrowth ideas.

The difficulty is, as the critic Frederick Jameson once noted, that "it is easier to imagine the end of the world than to imagine the end of capitalism". Take Joseph Stiglitz. He remains a fascinating critic of many things that are wrong both with the global economy and economics. He is also a good example of the reluctance, even among the more radical wing of what has been called even the "econocracy", to break with the old ways of thinking. His alternative is what he calls "progressive capitalism". It is not, he says, an oxymoron. Historically he is absolutely right, as we have seen. But is this right for the twenty-first century? Is it enough for it to say that "we can channel the power of the market to serve society", or is this an example that economists too can prefer economic "greenwash" to any deeper rethinking (Stiglitz 2019)?

Naomi Klein has suggested that

> our economy is at war with many forms of life on earth, including human life. What the climate needs to avoid collapse is a contraction in humanity's use of resources; what our economic model demands to avoid collapse is unfettered expansion. Only one set of these rules can be changed, and it is not the laws of nature.
>
> (Klein 2014: 21)

The need to go beyond the conventional endorsement of further productivity growth as a solution can also be seen when we look at the problems of global inequality.

## Can catch-up productivity work in the future?

In Chapters 6 and 7 we looked at more recent examples of catch-up productivity growth, their possibilities and their limits. We saw that some economies have made and are making the jump to higher levels of productivity and closing the gap with the advanced world. But others are stuck more or less on the lower rungs of the productivity ladder and there is a large group of economies still on the lowest rung. Yet mainstream views about how this might be changed also focus on trying to get more of the same in the future.

If this has not worked in the past, we need to ask why it could work in the future. This is partly an argument about global power structures. It is also an argument about the fallacy of composition. What if the levels of productivity that have been achieved in global capitalism are already so great as to swamp the possibilities of competitive growth in the rest of the world? The successes of productivity growth are such that today a much larger amount of output can be produced per worker than ever before. Labour productivity is now so great that no major economies in the future will be able to replicate the shares of labour in manufacturing that were once evident in Europe and the US. This is nothing to do with artificial intelligence and robotics. The shifting pattern is already evident in the data of the past half century.

The number of robots in use is still modest (Upchurch 2018). Hard materials seem to be easier for robots to deal with than soft, flimsy ones that easily pull out of shape. This is good for those who work in textiles, but although the numbers employed in the global textile sector have risen they are concentrated in a few countries. They are still a small part of the global labour force not least because the machinery they use, even if more limited than in some other sectors, has improved over time. Even second-hand sewing machines can be used to stitch more clothes per worker than in the past.

But when we do look towards more developed sectors, the ones that deliver the higher productivity gains and to which poor countries aspire to, then labour-saving technology becomes even more important. In 2015 one-third of industrial robot exports went to middle-income countries for car and electronic production, with China the largest importer. Even if we could imagine a scenario where an ever larger number of cars and electronic products could be consumed then this might not generate much employment at all. Worse, if robots are the future, then there might not be any advantage in putting them in poor countries, especially given their weak infrastructures. China aside, most robots are bought by the already rich countries, not the poorest ones (Bland 2016).

The fallacy of composition also undermines the argument that competitive catch-up productivity growth is the solution in another way. As we pointed out in Chapter 5, it assumes levels of output and resource use that are inconceivable save in a fantasy future where another planet like Mars becomes a new colony for humans to plunder. David Woodward, an economist working for the United Nations (and at one point an adviser on Africa), has called this idea *incrementum ad absurdum*. It is absurd because for poor countries raising *average* standards requires them to be chasing a moving target. But Woodward points out that even if we think in terms of releasing people from some more basic poverty level – say $1, or a more ambitious $5, a day – then because of the unequal distribution of the rewards, it would take 100 years to do the first and 200 years to do the second. None of this would address the issue of relative poverty at all, and even these modest targets would require unimaginable levels of total planetary output (Woodward 2015).

So, when we look beyond the advanced world we arrive back at the same point: the need for a more fundamental rethink of economic relations and the role of productivity change within them.

## Productivity and redistribution

Imagine an isolated island with 1,000 people. If the productivity level is so low that our island people can only produce 300 pairs of shoes, then there will always be a class of those with shoes and a class without shoes. The numbers in the shoeless class will be bigger if some people grab several pairs. But however we divide the shoes, we cannot avoid having a class of "shoe haves" and a class of "shoe have nots". Higher productivity potentially solves this problem. It may allow our island people to produce, say, 1,200 pairs of shoes. A minority can still grab a bigger share of the shoes. Then most will have one pair and some still none. But this is a distributional "choice". It is no longer the case that there has to be a class of those with shoes and another class without them. The rich countries have already made this productivity jump. Their productivity levels are so high that for a long time inequality has not been a product of insufficient production but the way production is allocated. At a global level too, productivity, although uneven, is already so high that it is possible to imagine ways of redistribution that could already massively improve the conditions of the global poor without negatively impacting on the mass of people in the richer countries. Let us stay with our shoe example. How many shoes does the global shoe industry produce each year? The answer is some 23 billion: this is enough for three pairs per person. The fact that people are still barefoot is therefore a testament not to low productivity but the unresolved issue of distribution.

One part of the problem is those at the very top. Their cupboards are full of high-end shoes. Some collect their Jimmy Choos as a sign of sophistication and wealth. They can do so because not only are the gains of productivity growth unequally shared, they have also become more unequal. Each year Oxfam publishes figures contrasting the wealth at the top with the poverty at the bottom. At the start of 2019 it estimated that the richest 26 people on the planet owned as much as the bottom 3.8 billion. The gap between what is and what could be is greater than it has ever been. Thomas Pogge has put it this way: "The really relevant comparison of existing poverty is not with historical benchmarks but with present possibilities. How much of this poverty is really avoidable today? By this standard our generation is doing worse than any in human history" (quoted in Hickel 2017: 47).

But this issue of redistribution raises uncomfortable issues. Critics point quite correctly to the problem of the global 1 per cent. But it is less often pointed out that to get into the top 1 per cent of the global income distribution you need to be earning, in British terms, roughly around £25,000–30,000 a year (it partly depends on the exchange rate). Most teachers in the advanced world are therefore part of the global 1 per cent. University lecturers certainly are. As for professors; well, perhaps it is best not to ask. So, while we need to rethink how unequal distribution rewards the very few, we also have to look beyond them as well. When I thought of my shoe example, I counted how many pairs I have. Including garden shoes, slippers, trainers, those on the way out and those never worn they numbered an embarrassing 18 pairs. Of course, it is far more than a question of individuals. Few of us get an opportunity to make any real decisions in the companies and institutions for which we work and in the societies in which we live. Despite the pairs of shoes that I have, and a posh title, I have spent most of my life following orders in a world into which I have had little input. You may feel the same. But that too is an argument about distribution: the distribution of productivity and power as both an input and an output.

This is where an argument about using future productivity gains to get different types of improvements – to get less from even less and then to redistribute not only within countries but between them – becomes more difficult. This book has tried to show how the debate on productivity is limited by its failure to look beyond its current narrow confines. I have not tried to write a polemic for a new kind of future but rather to show how the need for this is immanent in our current productivity dilemmas. Could such a future come into being?

If it does not it will not be because the possibilities are not there. Productivity gives us these: the issue is the determination with which these possibilities are seized. History points to two things that are positive. One is that we have not always been on the productivity treadmill. The treadmill has developed in the last 500 years and intensified in the last 100. But humans have been around for much longer. The second is that in other circumstances it has been possible to shift priorities. It is now pointed out – even by economists like Joseph Stiglitz – that in wartime economies can be shifted in completely new directions. This has happened not only to production but also to consumption. In the Second World War, for example, instead of marketing and advertising being designed to get people to want ever more, its focus became what is now called "demarketing": reducing demand and changing the pattern of demand. In Britain, despite the problems, this even led to more equality and better health outcomes.

This at least shows that it can be done. Huge changes have been made in a short time before. Whether they will be done in the future depends on many things, but one of them is challenging the view that productivity growth can allow things to go on as they are. Productivity is important, as we said at the start, but it is not always important in the way in which it is conventionally thought about. To understand its real significance we have had to unravel the productivity concept, explore the peculiarities of its mismeasurement and then follow its actual patterns across the globe to its future limits. We will only succeed in the next decades if we escape the limits of our past and present productivity obsessions.

# Bibliography

A number of large international data sets are now available that are valuable for the issues discussed in this book. Angus Maddison's original data sets (referred to here as the Maddison database) are all online and curated by the Groningen Growth and Development Centre (https://www.rug.nl/ggdc/), which continues his work and has generated valuable data sets of its own as well as acting as a portal to the other sources of data. Historical data are also available via the Clio-Infra project (https://clio-infra.eu/) linked to the OECD's Better Life Initiative. The US Conference Board (https://www.conference-board.org/data/economydatabase/) is the initial place to go to for modern global data. Each spring it publishes an updated comparative productivity brief and summary tables from its Total Economy Database. In our tables this is referred to as the US Conference Board. The OECD is a major source of data. The UN has a number of databases that usually go back to 1950: its World Urbanization Prospects are especially useful (https://population.un.org/wup/). The World Bank has created the increasingly detailed World Development Indicators. Some non-governmental organizations are creating valuable databases, for example the Global Footprint Network. Some databases have also been developed by companies, not least BP with the database for its annual Statistical Review of World Energy. However, readers need (as Chapter 3 suggests) to be continually alert to the issues of data quality.

Abramovitz, M. 1986. "Catching up, forging ahead, and falling behind". *Journal of Economic History* 46(2): 385–406.

Acemoglu, D. and J. Robinson 2012. *Why Nations Fail: The Origins of Power, Prosperity and Poverty*. London: Profile.

*Africa's Pulse* 2018. *Africa's Pulse: An Analysis of Issues Shaping Africa's Economic Future*. No. 18. Washington, DC: World Bank.

Akinyoade, A. and C. Uche 2016. *Dangote Cement: An African Success Story?* ASC Working Paper 131, African Studies Centre, Leiden.

Alesina, A. and D. Rodrik 1994. "Distributive politics and economic growth". *Quarterly Journal of Economics* 109(2): 465–90.

Allen, R. 2003. *Farm to Factory: A Reinterpretation of the Soviet Industrial Revolution*. Princeton, NJ: Princeton University Press.

Allen, R. 2011. *Global Economic History: A Very Short Introduction*. Oxford: Oxford University Press.

Allen, R. 2017. "Lessons from history for the future of work". *Nature News* 550 (7676): 321.

Amsden, A. 2001. *The Rise of "The Rest": Challenges to the West from Late-Industrializing Economies*. Oxford: Oxford University Press.

Andrews, D., C. Criscuolo & P. Gal 2016. "The global productivity slowdown, technology divergence and public policy: a firm level perspective". Background Paper for OECD Global Forum on Productivity.

Antonopoulos, R. 2008. "The unpaid care work paid work connection". The Levy Economics Institute working papers, no. 541, Levy Economics Institute of Bard College, Annandale-on-Hudson, New York.

Assa, J. 2017. *The Financialization of GDP: Implications for Economic Theory and Policy*. Abingdon: Routledge.

Atkinson, A. 2009. "Factor shares: the principal problem of political economy?" *Oxford Review of Economic Policy* 25(1): 3–16.

Austin, G. 2008. "Resources, techniques, and strategies south of the Sahara: Revising the factor endowments perspective on African economic development, 1500–2000". *Economic History Review* 61(3): 587–624.

Ayuba, K. and M. Haynes 2017. "Business and economics in Africa: one story or many?" *International Journal of Management Concepts and Philosophy* 10(1): 54–72.

Basu, K. 2018. "A short history of India's economy: a chapter in the Asian drama". United Nations WIDER Working Paper 2018/124.

Baumol, W. 1968. "Entrepreneurship in economic theory". *American Economic Review* 58(2): 64–71.

Baumol, W. 1990. "Entrepreneurship: productive, unproductive, and destructive". *Journal of Political Economy*, 98(5): 893–921.

Baumol, W. 2002. "Entrepreneurship, innovation and growth: the David–Goliath symbiosis". *Journal of Entrepreneurial Finance* 7(2): 1–10.

Baumol, W. 2012. *The Cost Disease: Why Computers Get Cheaper and Health Care Doesn't*. New Haven, CT: Yale University Press.

Baumol, W. and W. Bowen 1966. *Performing Arts: The Economic Dilemma*. New York: Twentieth Century Fund.

Bayart, J.-F. and S. Ellis 2000. "Africa in the world: a history of extraversion". *African Affairs* 99(395): 217–67.

Bhaumik, S. 2011. "Productivity and the economic cycle". UK Department for Business Innovation and Skills, BIS economics paper, no. 12, March.

Bland, B. 2016. "China's robot revolution". *Financial Times*, 6 June.

Blaug, M. 2001. "Is competition such a good thing? Static efficiency versus dynamic efficiency". *Review of Industrial Organization* 19(1): 37–48.

Block, F. 2008. "Swimming against the current: the rise of a hidden developmental state in the United States". *Politics & Society* 36(2): 169–206.

Bosworth, B. and S. Collins 2008. "Accounting for growth: comparing China and India". *Journal of Economic Perspectives* 22(1): 45–66.

Bresnahan, T. and M. Trajtenberg 1995. "General purpose technologies 'engines of growth'?" *Journal of Econometrics* 65(1): 83–108.

Broadberry, S. 1998. "How did the United States and Germany overtake Britain? A sectoral analysis of comparative productivity levels, 1870–1990". *Journal of Economic History* 58(2): 375–407.

Broadberry, S. 2006. *Market Services and the Productivity Race 1890–2000*. Cambridge: Cambridge University Press.

Broadberry, S., B. Campbell & B. van Leeuwen 2013. "When did Britain industrialise? The sectoral distribution of the labour force and labour productivity in Britain, 1381–1851". *Explorations in Economic History* 50(1): 16–27.

Brynjolfsson, E., D. Rock & C. Syverson 2017. "Artificial intelligence and the modern productivity paradox: a clash of expectations and statistics". NBER working paper no. 24001, November.

CDP UK 2017. *The Carbon Majors Database: CDP Carbon Majors Report 2017*. London: CDP UK.

Chang, H.-J. 2002. *Kicking Away the Ladder: Development Strategy in Historical Perspective*. London: Anthem Press.

Chang, H.-J. 2011. *23 Things They Don't Tell You About Capitalism*. London: Penguin.

Clark, J. 1891. "Distribution as determined by a law of rent". *Quarterly Journal of Economics* 5: 289–318.

Collier, P. 2007. *The Bottom Billion: Why the Poorest Countries are Failing and What Can Be Done About It*. Oxford: Oxford University Press.

Collier, P. 2009. *Wars, Guns and Votes: Democracy in Dangerous Places*. London: Bodley Head.

Coyle, D. 2015. *GDP: A Brief but Affectionate History*. Princeton, NJ: Princeton University Press.

Crafts, N. 2017. "Whither economic growth?" *Finance and Development* 54(1): 3–6.

Crafts, N. and G. Toniolo (eds) 1996. *Economic Growth in Europe since 1945*. Cambridge: Cambridge University Press.

Daly, H. 2007. *Ecological Economics and Sustainable Development: Selected Essays of Herman Daly*. Cheltenham: Edward Elgar.

Daly, H. 2005. "Economics in a full world". *Scientific American* 293(3): 100–7.

Daly, H. and B. Kunkel 2018. "Ecologies of scale". *New Left Review* 109: 81–104.

Davies, R. 1998. *Soviet Economic Development From Lenin to Khrushchev*. Cambridge: Cambridge University Press.

Davis, E. 2011. *Made in Britain*. London: Little, Brown.

Davis, M. 2006. *Planet of Slums*. London: Verso.

De Haan, M. and J. Haynes 2018. "R & D capitalisation: where did we go wrong?" *Eurostat Review of National Accounts and Macroeconomic Indicators* 1: 7–33.

De Jong, H. 2015. "Living standards in a modernizing world – a long-run perspective on material wellbeing and human development". *Global Handbook of Quality of Life*, 45–74. Dordrecht: Springer.

Denison, E. 1968. "Economic growth". In R. Caves (ed.), *Britain's Economic Prospects*. Washington, DC: Brookings Institution Press.

Despain, H. 2015. "Secular stagnation: mainstream versus Marxian traditions". *Monthly Review* 67(4): 39.

Diamond, J. 2005. "The shape of Africa". *National Geographic* 208(3): 22.

Dollar, D. 2018. "Is China's development finance a challenge to the international order?" *Asian Economic Policy Review* 13(2): 283–98.

Dorling, D. 2013. *Population 10 Billion*. London: Constable.

Dreze, J. and A. Sen 1990. *Hunger and Public Action*. Oxford: Clarendon Press.

Easterlin, R. 1974. "Does economic growth improve the human lot? Some empirical evidence". In *Nations and Households in Economic Growth: Essays in Honor of Moses Abramowitz*. New York: Academic Press.

Ebenstein, L. 2015. *Chicagonomics: The Evolution of Chicago Free Market Economics*. New York: St. Martin's Press.

Enache, M., E. Ghani & S. O'Connell 2016. *Structural Transformation in Africa: A Historical View*. World Bank Policy Research working paper 7743.

Federico, G. 2005. *Feeding the World: An Economic History of Agriculture, 1800–2000*, Princeton, NJ: Princeton University Press.

French, H. 2005. *A Continent for the Taking: The Tragedy and Hope of Africa*. London: Vintage.

Fuglie, K. and N. Rada 2013. *Resources, Policies, and Agricultural Productivity in Sub-Saharan Africa*. Washington, DC: US Department of Agriculture.

Garcia-Macia, D., C.-T. Hsieh & P. Klenow 2016. "How destructive is innovation?" NBER Working Paper Series, no. 22953.

GFC 2017. *Financing Investment: Interim Report*. GFC Consulting, London, 11 December.

Gordon, R. 2015. "Secular stagnation: a supply-side view". *American Economic Review* 105(5): 54–9.

Gordon, R. 2016. *The Rise and Fall of American Growth: The US Standard of Living Since the Civil War*. Princeton, NJ: Princeton University Press.

Gould, J. 1972. *Economic Growth in History*. London: Methuen.

Graeber, D. 2018. *Bullshit Jobs: A Theory*. London: Penguin.

Habakkuk, H. 1962. *American and British Technology in the Nineteenth Century: The Search for Labour-Saving Inventions*. Cambridge: Cambridge University Press.

Hahn, F. and R. Matthews 1965. "The theory of economic growth: a survey". In *Surveys of Economic Theory: Growth and Development*. London: Macmillan.

Haldane, A. 2017. "Productivity puzzles". Bank of England, London, 20 March.

Haldane, A. 2018. "The UK's productivity problem: hub no spokes". Bank of England, London, 28 June.

Haldane, A. and B. Nelson 2012. "Tails of the unexpected". Bank of England, London, 8 June.

Hall, S. (with B. Schwarz) 2017. *Familiar Stranger: A Life Between Two Islands*. London: Allen Lane.

Hammond, R. 2014. "Life in Lagos: in search of the African middle class". *National Geographic*, 19 December.

Handelsbatt Research Institute 2017. *The Future of Farming and Food*. Leverkusen: Bayer.

Harvey, D. 2004. "The 'new' imperialism: accumulation by dispossession". *Socialist Register* 40: 63–87.

Hausman, J. 1997. "Valuation of new goods under perfect and imperfect competition". In T. Bresnahan & R. Gordon (eds), *The Economics of New Goods*. Chicago, IL: University of Chicago Press.

Haynes, M. 2017. "Soviet history, red globalization and the political economy of global capitalism". *Journal of Contemporary Central and Eastern Europe* 25(1): 135–48.

Heintz, J. 2019. *The Economy's Other Half: How Taking Gender Seriously Transforms Macroeconomics*. Newcastle upon Tyne: Agenda Publishing.

Hickel, J. 2017. *The Divide: A Brief Guide to Global Inequality and its Solutions*. London: Heinemann.

Hobsbawm, E. 1962. *The Age of Revolution: Europe 1789–1848*. London: Weidenfeld & Nicolson.

Huberman, M. and C. Minns 2005. "Hours of work in Old and New Worlds: the long view, 1870–2000". Institute of International Integration Studies discussion paper 95.

Huberman, M. and C. Minns 2007. "The times they are not changin': days and hours of work in Old and New Worlds, 1870–2000". *Explorations in Economic History* 44(4): 538–67.

Hulten, C. 2001. "Total factor productivity: a short biography". In C. Hulten, E. Dean & M. Harper (eds), *New Developments in Productivity Analysis*, 1–54. Chicago, IL: University of Chicago Press.

ILO 2019. *The Future of Work in Textiles, Clothing, Leather and Footwear.* Geneva: International Labour Organisation.

Jerven, M. 2013. *Poor Numbers: How We Are Misled by African Development Statistics and What to Do About It.* Cornell, NY: Cornell University Press.

Jerven, M. 2015. *Africa: Why Economists Get It Wrong.* London: Zed Books.

Jevons, W. 1906. [1865]. *The Coal Question: An Inquiry Concerning the Progress of the Nation, and the Probable Exhaustion of our Coal-Mines,* Third edition. London: Macmillan.

Jones, N. 2018. "How to stop data centres from gobbling up the world's electricity". *Nature,* 12 September.

Kallis, G. 2018. *Degrowth.* Newcastle upon Tyne: Agenda Publishing.

Kanefsky, J. 1979. "Motive power in British industry and the accuracy of the 1870 Factory Returns". *Economic History Review* 32(3): 360–75.

Kentikelenis, A., T. Stubbs & L. King 2016. "IMF conditionality and development policy space, 1985–2014". *Review of International Political Economy* 23(4): 543–82.

Kenyes, J. 1930 [1931]. "The economic possibilities for our grandchildren". In J. Keynes, *Essays in Persuasion.* London: Macmillan.

Klein, N. 2014. *This Changes Everything: Capitalism vs. The Climate.* New York: Simon & Schuster.

Komlos, J. 2016. "Has creative destruction become more destructive?" *BE Journal of Economic Analysis & Policy* 16(4): np.

Krueger, A. and T. Taylor 2000. "An interview with Zvi Griliches". *Journal of Economic Perspectives* 14(2): 171–89.

Krugman, P. 1994a. *The Age of Diminished Expectations.* Cambridge, MA: MIT Press.

Krugman, P. 1994b. "The myth of Asia's miracle". *Foreign Affairs* 76(6): 62–78.

Kukah, M. 1999. *Democracy and Civil Society in Nigeria.* Ibadan, Nigeria: Spectrum Books.

Kuznets, S. 1955. "Economic growth and income inequality". *American Economic Review* 45(1): 1–28.

Landefeld, S., E. Seskin & B. Fraumeni 2008. "Taking the pulse of the economy: measuring GDP". *Journal of Economic Perspectives* 22(2): 193–216.

Layard, R. 2011. *Happiness: Lessons From a New Science.* London: Penguin.

Lee, J.-W. and H. Lee 2016. "Human capital in the long run". *Journal of Development Economics* 122(C): 147–69.

Lepenies, P. 2016. *The Power of a Single Number: A Political History of GDP.* New York: Columbia University Press.

Levitt, S. and S. Dubner 2015. *When to Rob a Bank: The Freakopedia.* London: Allen Lane.

Lipsey, R. and K. Lancaster 1956. "The general theory of second best". *Review of Economic Studies* 24(1): 11–32.

Lucas, R. 2004. "Macroeconomic priorities". *American Economic Review* 93(1): 1–14.

Lucas, R. 2004. "The industrial revolution: past and future". *The Region* (2003 Annual Report of the Federal Reserve Bank of Minneapolis): 5–20.

McKinsey 2012. *Meet the 2020 Chinese Consumer.* McKinsey Insights China.

McMillan, M., D. Rodrik & I. Verduzco-Gallo 2014. "Globalization, structural change, and productivity growth, with an update on Africa". *World Development* 63: 11–32.

Marglin, S. 2010. *The Dismal Science: How Thinking Like an Economist Undermines Community*. Cambridge, MA: Harvard University Press.

Mazzucato, M. 2013. *The Entrepreneurial State: Debunking Public Versus Private Sector Myths*. London: Anthem Press.

Mazzucato, M. 2018a. *The Value of Everything: Making and Taking in the Global Economy*. London: Penguin.

Mazzucato, M. 2018b. "Who really creates value in an economy? The billionaires, or us?" *Project Syndicate*, 13 September.

Medina, L., A. Jonelis & M. Cabgul 2016. "The informal economy on Sub-Saharan Africa: size and determinants". IMF Working Paper WP/17/156.

Milanovic, B. 2016. *Global Inequality: A New Approach for the Age of Globalization*. Cambridge, MA: Harvard University Press.

Morgenstern, O. 1963. *On the Accuracy of Economic Observations*. Second edition. Princeton, NJ: Princeton University Press.

Musson, A. 1976. "Industrial motive power in the UK, 1800–1870". *Economic History Review* 29(3): 415–39.

Ndikumana, L. 2017. *Curtailing Capital Flight from Africa*. Berlin: Friedrich-Ebert-Stiftung.

Newfarmer, R., J. Page & F. Tarp (eds) 2019. *Industries without Smokestacks: Industrialization in Africa Reconsidered*. Oxford: Oxford University Press.

Nordhaus, W. 1973. "The allocation of energy reserves". *Brookings Papers* on *Economic Activity* 3: 529–70.

OECD 2001. *Measuring Productivity: Measurement of Aggregate and Industry-Level Productivity Growth*. OECD Manual. Paris: OECD.

OECD 2014. *How Was Life? Global Well Being Since 1820*. OECD: Paris.

Persaud, A. 2017. "London: the money laundering capital of the world". *Prospect*, 27 April.

Peston, R. 2017. *WTF?* London: Hodder.

Pigou, A. 1932. *The Economics of Welfare*. Fourth edition. London: Macmillan.

Piketty, T. 2014. *Capital in the Twenty-First Century*. Cambridge, MA: Harvard University Press.

Pilling, D. 2018a. *The Growth Delusion: The Wealth and Well-Being of Nations*. London: Bloomsbury.

Pilling, D. 2018b. "African economy: the limits of 'leapfrogging'". *Financial Times*, 13 August.

Poonam, S. 2019. *Dreamers: How Young Indians Are Changing the World*. London: Hurst.

Pullinger, J. 1997. "The Creation of the Office for National Statistics". *International Statistical Review/Revue Internationale de Statistique* 65(3): 291–308.

Raworth, K. 2018. *Doughnut Economics: Seven Ways to Think Like a 21st Century Economist*. London: Penguin.

Raynes, R. and I. Nair 1984. "Thermodynamics and economics". *Physics Today* 37(11): 62–71.

Reinsberg, B. *et al.* 2019. "The world system and the hollowing out of state capacity: how structural adjustment programs affect bureaucratic quality in developing countries". *American Journal of Sociology* 124(4): 1222–57.

Rodrik, D. 2005. "Growth strategies". In P. Aghion & S. Durlauf (eds), *Handbook of Economic Growth*, volume 1A. Amsterdam: Elsevier.

Rodrik, D. 2007. *One Economics, Many Recipes: Globalization, Institutions and Economic Growth*. Princeton, NJ: Princeton University Press.

Romer, P. 1994. "The origins of endogenous growth". *Journal of Economic Perspectives* 8(1): 3–22.

Romer, P. 1996. "Why, indeed, in America? Theory, history, and the origins of modern economic growth". NBER Working Paper No. 5443.

Rostow, W. 1960. *The Stages of Economic Growth: A Non-Communist Manifesto*. Cambridge: Cambridge University Press.

Schumpeter, J. 1976 [1943]. *Capitalism, Socialism and Democracy*. London: Allen & Unwin.

Selwyn, B. 2011. "Liberty limited? A sympathetic re-engagement with Amartya Sen's *Development as Freedom*". *Economic and Political Weekly* 46(37): 68–76.

Selwyn, B. 2014. *The Global Development Crisis*. Cambridge: Polity.

Selwyn, B. 2018. "Poverty chains and global capitalism". *Competition and Change* 23(1): 71–97.

Shane, S. 2008. *The Illusions of Entrepreneurship: The Costly Myths that Entrepreneurs, Investors and Policy Makers Live by*. New Haven, CT: Yale University Press.

Simms, A. 2016. "It's the economy that needs to be integrated into the environment – not the other way around". *Guardian*, 4 June.

Siyi, H. and Z. Ying 2019. "Invest to innovate". *China Report* 73: 33–5.

Smith, A. 1970. [1776]. *The Wealth of Nations. Books 1–111*. Harmondsworth: Penguin.

Solow, R. 1956. "A contribution to the theory of economic growth". *Quarterly Journal of Economics* 70(1): 65–94.

Solow, R. 1986. "On the intergenerational allocation of natural resources". *Scandinavian Journal of Economics* 88(1): 141–9.

Standing, G. 2016. *The Corruption of Capitalism: Why Rentiers Thrive and Work Does Not Pay*. London: Biteback.

Stern, N. 2008. "The economics of climate change". *American Economic Review* 98(2): 1–37.

Stiglitz, J. 2002. *Globalization and its Discontents*. New York: Norton.

Stiglitz, J. 2014. "Stagnation by design". *Project Syndicate*, 6 February.

Stiglitz, J. 2019. *People, Power, and Profits: Progressive Capitalism for an Age of Discontent*. London: Allen Lane.

Subramanian, A. 2019. "India's GDP mis-estimation: likelihood, magnitudes, mechanisms, and implications". Center for International Development, Harvard University, working paper No. 354.

Syverson, C. 2004. "Product substitutability and productivity dispersion". *Review of Economics and Statistics* 86(2): 534–50.

Syverson, C. 2017. "Challenges to mismeasurement explanations of the US productivity slowdown". *Journal of Economic Perspectives* 31(3): 165–86.

Tawney, R. 1921. *The Acquisitive Society*. London: Bell.

Temin, P. 2002. "The golden age of European growth reconsidered". *European Review of Economic History* 6(1): 3–22.

Thirlwall, A. 1983. "A plain man's guide to Kaldor's growth laws". *Journal of Post-Keynesian Economics* 5(3): 345–58.

Tobin, J. 1977. "How dead is Keynes?" *Economic Inquiry* 15(4): 459–68.

Turner, A. 2016. *Between Debt and the Devil: Money, Credit and Fixing Global Finance*. Princeton, NJ: Princeton University Press.

United Nations 2009. *System of National Accounts 2008*. New York: United Nations.

Upchurch, M. 2018. "Robots and AI at work: the prospects for singularity". *New Technology, Work and Employment* 33(3): 205–18.

Wade, R. 2003. "What strategies are viable for developing countries today? The World Trade Organization and the shrinking of 'development space'". *Review of International Political Economy* 10(4): 621–44.

Wei, S.-J., Z. Xie & X. Zhang 2017. "From 'made in China' to 'innovated in China': necessity, prospect, and challenges". *Journal of Economic Perspectives* 31(1): 49–70.

Woodward, D. 2015. "Incrementum ad absurdum: global growth, inequality and poverty eradication in a carbon-constrained world". *World Economic Review* 4: 43–62.

World Bank 1993. *The East Asian Miracle: Economic Growth and Public Policy*. New York: Oxford University Press.

World Trade Organization 2018. *Global Value Chain Development Report 2017. Measuring and Analyzing the Impact of GVCs on Economic Development*. Geneva: World Trade Organization.

Xiaodong, Y. 2019. "Choosing the right road". *China Report* 73: 16–19.

# Index